CLASSIC FILMS

Classic Films - Famous and Forgotten Films
Volume One

Written by Constance Metzinger

Published by Lantz Publishing Ltd.
North Olmsted, Ohio
1 3 5 7 9 10 8 6 4 2

This edition copyright ©2025 Lantz Publishing Ltd.
All Rights Reserved.

ISBN 13: 978-1-945701-24-5

CLASSIC FILMS

VOLUME ONE
Edition

CONSTANCE METZINGER
Editor

Feature Pictures

ROME EXPRESS (1932)	9
BEAUTY FOR SALE (1933)	11
THE PRIVATE LIFE OF HENRY VIII (1933)	17
THE LITTLE MINISTER (1934)	21
NAUGHTY MARIETTA (1935)	25
THE ADVENTURES OF ROBIN HOOD (1938)	32
LISTEN DARLING (1938)	40
THE FOUR FEATHERS (1939)	45
HOLD THAT GHOST! (1941)	49
THE WOLF MAN 1941)	53
ABOVE SUSPICION (1942)	59
ASSIGNMENT IN BRITTANY (1943)	63
LES ANGES DU PECHE (1943)	67
ROAD TO UTOPIA (1945)	73
CINDERELLA (1947)	77

The Ghost and Mrs. Muir (1947) 80
The Luck of the Irish (1948) 87
The Secret Garden (1948) 93
The Small Back Room (1949) 97
Broken Arrow (1950) 100
Stage Fright (1950) 105
Anna (1951) 111
Darling, How Could You! (1951) 114
Mr. Belvedere Rings the Bell (1951) 118
The River (1951) 125
Scaramouche (1952) 129
All I Desire (1953) 133
Titanic (1953) 137
Brigadoon (1954) 141
Picnic (1955) 147
Beyond a Reasonable Doubt (1956) 155
Omar Khayyam (1957) 157
The Buccaneer (1958) 160
The 7th Voyage of Sinbad (1958) 165
Darby O'Gill and the Little People (1959) 171
Edge of Eternity (1959) 175
The Shaggy Dog (1959) 179

A Majority of One (1961) 184
The Miss Marple Mysteries 190
The Sword in the Stone (1963) 203
The Moon-Spinners (1963) 206
Robinson Crusoe on Mars (1964) 210
The Ghost and Mr. Chicken (1966) 215
How to Steal a Million (1966) 221
Half a Sixpence (1967) 225
The Prime of Miss Jean Brodie (1969) 229
Les Deux Anglaises (1971) 235
Mr. Forbush and the Penguins (1971) 241
The Golden Voyage of Sinbad (1974) 245
The Island at the Top of the World (1974) 248
The Tamarind Seed (1974) 253
The Getting of Wisdom (1977) 257
Nugget Reviews .... 44, 96, 174, and 228

An Introduction

Back in the 2010s, Turner Classic Movies — better known as TCM — operated an online fan club called the TCM Classic Film Union. It was a wonderful site where classic film lovers could interact, share, and discover "new" old movies. One of the most popular sections of the site was the community blogs, where regular fans contributed in-depth film reviews. Reading other people's opinions of films that my sister Diana and I grew up with and loved inspired me to write my own reviews — a passion that eventually led to the creation of our own blog, *Silver Scenes*.

Writing reviews and sharing that love of classic film on *Silver Scenes* has been a pleasurable hobby for me for over ten years. During that time, I have reviewed several hundred films, ranging from the universally acclaimed classics to rarities that have long been forgotten. Other critics and bloggers can cover the famous films; it is the rare and unheralded classics that I truly enjoy sharing. As a result, *Silver Scenes* has come to focus on these hidden gems, which include many from studios outside Hollywood, such as those of Great Britain, Australia, Italy, Germany, and France.

There are thousands of classic films waiting to be reviewed, and the more I watch, the more titles I discover — which means the list of films I want to share with you keeps growing! Since *Silver Scenes* is a small blog with a limited readership, it seemed about the right time to get some of these reviews into book form. Hence, the book you are holding is the first of — hopefully — a multi-volume series of paperbacks covering the classics... the famous and the forgotten.

And just what is a "classic"? If a film was made before 1970, then in my book it deserves that title — regardless of how good or bad the film is. A better definition of a true classic is a film that generations of fans have enjoyed (it holds up well over repeated viewings) and one that features all the elements of great filmmaking: good acting, a strong script, and quality production. Fortunately, classics are plentiful.

I hope you enjoy the selection of film reviews featured in this first volume and, more importantly, I hope you discover a new favorite through this book.

Enjoy!

Constance Metzinger

You can check out Silver Scenes online by visiting:
https://silverscenesblog.blogspot.com

CLASSIC FILMS

Famous *and* Forgotten Films

Volume 1

GAINSBOROUGH STUDIOS (1932)

ROME EXPRESS

"Romance and Adventure Roaring Through the Night!"

A valuable Van Dyck painting has been stolen from an art museum in Paris and the thief (Conrad Veidt) is onboard the Rome Express heading to Italy. This sinister criminal is in search of a Mr. Poole (Donald Calthrop) who snatched the painting from him in an attempt to double-cross him.

There is also a motley band of characters onboard the train whose lives will all intertwine with this criminal during the course of their journey to Rome. There is Asta Marvelle (Esther Ralston) a beautiful American movie star; Alistair McBain (Cedric Hardwicke) a millionaire philanthropist who is traveling with his secretary Mills (Eliot Makeham); a pair of adulterous lovers (Harold Huth and Joan Barry); a golfing bore (Gordon Harker); and a beetle-hunting police chief (Frank Vosper).

Rome Express was one of the very first thrillers set on a train and it inspired a number of similarly themed films, including Alfred Hitchcock's *The Lady Vanishes* (1935). Walter Forde beautifully directed this taut little picture and utilized a number of innovative filming tricks including long panning shots and fast cuts between scenes, but what makes it truly stand out is its snappy dialogue by Frank Vosper and Sidney Gilliat who, not surprisingly, also penned the scripts to *The Lady Vanishes* and *Night Train to Munich* (1940).

Rome Express speeds along at a fast pace and is never tiresome. The ending could have been tied up a little more snugly but on the whole, it is good entertainment. The interactions between the various characters, most of whom are strangers to one another, drive the story forward and, in this respect, *Rome Express* is similar to *The Ghost Train* (1931), which, not surprisingly, was also directed by Walter Forde.

Conrad Veidt, who was making his English-speaking debut, is devilishly charming as the villain while Cedric Hardwicke is entertaining to watch as the penny-pinching philanthropist who delights in being demeaning to his secretary Mills. Also in the cast is Hugh Williams and Finlay Currie.

METRO-GOLDWYN-MAYER (1933)

Beauty for Sale

"I got a living to earn for two and I can't do it in Kentucky. You got to take your spoon where the soup is." - Letty

"Well, the soup's hot in New York, kid. You're likely to get burned." - Carol

Letty (Madge Evans) is a small-town girl who heads to New York City to work at Madame Sonia Barton's beauty salon. While there, she falls in love with Sherwood (Otto Kruger), the husband of one of her clients (Alice Brady). He does not want to divorce his wife and so Letty must decide whether to leave him or have a backstairs relationship with him for the rest of her life.

MGM's *Beauty for Sale* was one of many variations of the oft-used three-working-girls plot first popularized in *Sally, Irene, and Mary* in 1925. It was still fresh in the 1930s and by altering the setting MGM was able to reuse it successfully throughout the decade in other films, none quite as good as this one.

The three beauty parlor girls are played by Madge Evans, Una Merkel, and Florine McKinney, all of whom are low on lover's luck. Carol (Merkel) had a sour experience with real love that left her bitter and so she sets her eyes on catching a rich sugar daddy instead...which she does. Jane (McKinney) has fallen in love with Madame Sonia's son (Phillips Holmes) but is quickly abandoned when he learns she is pregnant.

Letty judges her relationship with Sherwood in the light of both of her friend's experiences and decides to part ways with him. She reluctantly returns to her hometown beau (Eddie Nugent) but quickly regrets this decision.

"I didn't make the world the way it is, but I gotta live in it."

A 1933 review from Variety magazine pegged *Beauty of Sale* perfectly: "Pulp magazine fiction made for subway-riding stenographers... romantic hoke skillfully dressed up."

It may be hoke, but mighty entertaining hoke it is! *Beauty for Sale* has a well-shaken blend of drama and comedy. It begins with sentimentality, reaches a dramatic climax, and then takes a sudden and brief dip into screwball comedy. This may sound like a potent mixture for an MGM film, yet the final result is quite pleasing. The film was the forerunner of the lush - and much more dramatic - melodramas of the 1950s (e.g. *Three Coins in a Fountain, The Best of Everything*), and like those films, even when you know the ending you can sit through them over and over again and still enjoy it.

"It's a pity mother didn't drown you as a pup!" - Carol

Eve Green and Zelda Sear's script, based on the Faith Baldwin novel "Beauty", is positively sparkling with wit. Una Merkel is given the best wisecracks, Alice Brady the most humorous lines, and Madge Evans has some of the sauciest remarks in the script. The direction, by Richard Boleslavsky (*Theodora Goes Wild*), is fast-paced and the cinematography is lovely. James Wong Howe used some clever angle shots and an abundance of soft-focus lenses. Madge Evans' close-ups are particularly beautiful.

Evans was one of the most irresistible actresses to ever come out of Hollywood. She was also one of only a handful of child stars to have made a successful transition into being a leading lady of the screen. Her pre-code films were her best and *Beauty for Sale* ranks as one of her most popular.

In 1933, Evans and Merkel were the most in-demand players on MGM's roster with Evans making 16 films between 1933 and 1934. Madge was often teamed with Robert Montgomery but she seems more enthralled by Otto Kruger than she ever was with Mr. Montgomery. They have wonderful on-screen chemistry together which is especially evident in one scene early in their relationship. Letty comes out of a restaurant during a thunderstorm and runs under a stoop only to bump into Sherwood. "There are only two things I am afraid of," she tells him, "thunderstorms and caterpillars!" Then a clap of thunder sends her flying into his arms.

Kruger is quite effective as the unassuming lover even though Edmund Lowe or Warren William could have made an equally charming Sherwood. The cast is a who's-who of recognizable 1930s film characters. Alice Brady plays one of her usual dithery society dames, Charley Grapewin has a great part as Carol's benevolent boyfriend, Hedda Hopper plays the lofty Madame Sonia, and the great May Robson has a wonderful part as the mother of Letty's hometown boyfriend, Bill.

LONDON FILMS (1933)

The Private Life of HENRY VIII

The name of Charles Laughton has become synonymous with that of King Henry VIII, a role that he portrayed both onscreen and on stage. Laughton was 34-years-old when he played the part of this beer-gulping, head-chopping monarch, and his delightfully raucous portrayal remains a highlight in a career of top-notch performances.

British film-maker Alexander Korda had his first international success with this peek into the "private life" of the oft-married monarch King Henry VIII. The picture should have been titled *The Private Loves of Henry VIII* for the focus of much of the film is on Henry's wives.

As the introductory written statement proclaims, "Henry VIII had six wives. Catherine of Aragon was the first; but her story is of no particular interest-- she was a respectable woman. So Henry divorced her."

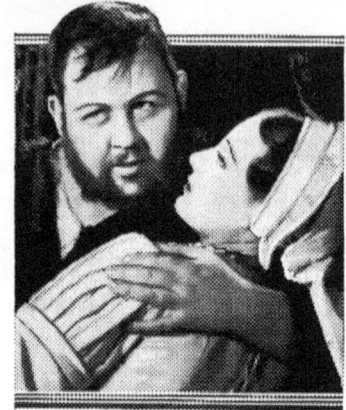

Charles Laughton and Binnie Barnes in The Private Life of Henry VIII

The film opens with Anne Boleyn (Merle Oberon), who is making preparations for her execution.

"Will the net hold my hair together when my head falls?" she asks.

Queens must think of the appearance they make to their subjects, even after death.

FAMOUS AND FORGOTTEN FILMS

Anne Boleyn knows her fate well enough. She recognizes the glances of affection that King Henry VIII (Charles Laughton) gives to Jane Seymour (Wendy Barrie) and realizes that his only course of action will be to have her put to death.... which he promptly does.

Poor Jane Seymour has a short tenure as the king's wife as well, but she at least dies a natural death. Then Henry spies the beautiful Katherine Howard (Binnie Barnes), a lady of the court. She is the object of affection for Squire Thomas (Robert Donat) but when she realizes that the king is smitten with her, she gladly sets her eyes upon the crown instead. Love is freely sacrificed to the god of ambition.

"Love eternal...since yesterday afternoon, until tomorrow morning?" - Katherine Howard

"When I say love, I mean love." - King Henry VIII

It is Katherine whom we are led to believe that the king loved the most among his many wives, but when he discovers her relationship with Squire Thomas, he nevertheless sets her head rolling. Anne of Cleves (Elsa Lancaster) and Katherine Parr (Everley Gregg) take turns wearing the band before Henry disgustedly exclaims in his old age, "Six wives - and the best of them was the worst of them."

The Private Life of Henry VIII is filled to the brim with delicious dialogue by Lajos Biro. The picture leans more toward satire than drama and it is this winning combination of humor amidst such serious British history that makes *The Private Life of Henry VIII* so novel and so very entertaining. It was one of the first films from England to become successful in America and throughout Europe. With his earnings from the production, Alexander Korda went on to launch London Films, one of England's most prestigious film studios.

In spite of the plot's focus on the wives of the enormous monarch, it is King Henry himself who takes center-stage throughout the film due to the magnificent presence of Charles Laughton. The actor bears a striking resemblance to the real Henry and his mannerisms most certainly must have matched that of the king. Nearly twenty years later, he would play King Henry VIII again in *Young Bess* (1953).

In fact, the entire casting for *The Private Life of Henry VIII* was excellent. Binnie Barnes gives an alluring performance as Katherine Howard and Merle Oberon, too, makes an impression even with such a brief appearance. Elsa Lancaster has a wonderful part as one of the few wives that Henry did not bed. Her clever method of remaining a virgin is one of the most amusing scenes in the film. And lastly, dear Robert Donat gives a rare supporting role and offers a hint to the audience of what a great leading man he will soon become.

Also in the cast is John Loder, Miles Mander, William Austin and Lady Tree.

RKO (1934)

THE LITTLE MINISTER

The Little Minister is a charming film about a recently ordained minister (John Beal) of a small Scottish village who gets rebuffed by his congregation when he falls in love with a wild gypsy girl (Katharine Hepburn).

At first, he wins the respect of the townsfolk when he stands up against the town bully Rob Dow (Alan Hale). Dow is the leader of the village weavers who are planning a rebellion against their employer, Lord Rintoul (Frank Convoy), who has cut their salary.

But, when the minister brazenly associates with Babbie, the sprightly gypsy of the woods, and announces his plans to marry her, he is practically tarred and feathered before it is found out that she is really the illustrious Lady Babbie, ward to Lord Rintoul, in disguise.

Sir James M. Barrie's whimsical tale "The Little Minister" was beloved by the masses since its first publication as a novel in 1891. The famous American stage star Maude Adams made the play a huge success in England and America. In 1921, both Paramount and Vitagraph released film versions of *The Little Minister* starring Betty Compson and Alice Calhoun, respectively.

Katharine Hepburn had always adored Maude Adams and when she heard that RKO was planning to make *The Little Minister* a major production with Ginger Rogers in the lead role, she was anxious to secure the part of Lady Babbie herself. Pandro S. Berman, the head of RKO, was more than happy to cast her in the role, hoping to restore her to her star status after the dismal failure of her previous film, *Spitfire*.

The husband and wife team of Victor Heerman and Sarah Y. Mason were brought in to weave a screenplay that would parallel their Oscar-winning script of 1933 - *Little Women*. In fact, most of the production team of *Little Women* were reunited for *The Little Minister*, which RKO lavishly bestowed with a $648,000 budget. It was the studio's most expensive production of the year and was released as their Christmas gift to the nation. Berman was secretly hoping for a major success but alack and alas, the film did not regain its expenses. Even though it brought in respectable business, it lost $9000.

Katharine Hepburn considered her portrayal of Babbie as a "rather fancy performance" years later, looking back on the film. The role of Babbie called for a girl with an almost other-worldly elfin quality and "I think I'm probably just too down-to-earth for that," Hepburn admitted.

George Cukor, one of Hepburn's favorite directors, was busy making *David Copperfield* over at Metro-Goldwyn-Mayer, and could not be called upon to take the helm of *The Little Minister*. In his place, Richard Wallace (*The Shopworn Angel, Sinbad the Sailor*) did a marvelous job.

The film itself is an enchanting fantasy and from its opening scenes lures the audience into the picturesque village of Thrums. Max Steiner's lovely score, which incorporates old and familiar Scottish tunes, carries our hearts into the highland while RKO's resident wizards of design, Van Nest Poglase and Carroll Clark, lend the film a total sense of authenticity by way of their meticulous set designs. No expense was spared in making *The Little Minister* the high-class production that it was. In addition to the leading actors, Donald Crisp, Lumsden Hare, Andy Clyde, Dorothy Stickney, Reginald Denny, Eily Malyon, and Mary Gordon also starred.

METRO-GOLDWYN-MAYER (1935)

NAUGHTY MARIETTA

Jeanette MacDonald knew how to flaunt spunk like no other woman in her time and, incredibly, she reigned during an era of ultra-spunky women. Jeanette knew how to be feisty and flirty without losing any of her natural grace which made her ideal to play roles of princesses in the guise of commoners, a recurring theme in her films and one which began with *Naughty Marietta* (1935), the first picture to pair MacDonald with Nelson Eddy.

Who would have predicted that an old 1910 Victor Herbert operetta starring two relatively unknown film personalities would become the smash hit of 1935? Ah, sweet mystery of showbiz! Producer Hunt Stromberg evidently recognized the wealth to be found in this gem of a pairing. MacDonald and Eddy were such an engaging duo that audiences immediately loved the unique quality of their onscreen comradery, their playful banter, scrumptious singing voices, and their fetching good looks.

Naughty Marietta was hugely successful and established MacDonald and Eddy as the "Singing Sweethearts". Their first film together featured all of the special ingredients that would be included in each subsequent MacDonald/Eddy musical: adventure, romance, witty dialogue, humor, and beautiful music.

"For 'tis love, and love alone, the world is seeking"

CLASSIC FILMS

Jeanette MacDonald stars as Princess Marie of France, who is being pressured by her evil uncle (Douglas Dumbrille) to wed the foppish Don Carlos of Spain. To escape from this fate she swaps places with her maid, Marietta, and joins a shipload of casquette girls bound for America. Casquette girls were French women that were sent to the French colonies of Louisiana to be the wives of colonists.

Just as they approach Louisiana, the women are captured by a band of pirates and dragged to their lair in the swamps. It is the dashing Captain Warrington (Nelson Eddy), leader of a troop of mercenaries who comes to their rescue. *Hoorah for Captain Warrington!* He quickly recognizes the regal quality of Marietta's bearing but has no inkling that she is a princess in disguise. Instead, smitten with her charms, he begins to woo her and within thirty minutes of film time she falls for his winsome ways.... as does the audience.

Naughty Marietta is pure entertainment from start to finish and justly deserved its Best Picture Oscar nomination that year. If the script seems to have that added sparkle it is because it was penned by the husband-and-wife team of Albert Hackett and Frances Goodrich, whose work included *The Thin Man* series and the film *Seven Brides for Seven Brothers*.

Victor Herbert's beautiful musical numbers included "Ah, Sweet Mystery of Life"

(which became MacDonald's signature song), "Italian Street Song", "Chansonette", "Tramp Tramp Tramp" and the lovely "I'm Falling in Love with Someone".

MacDonald and Eddy were not only talented singers but adroit comedians as well. The "'Neath the Southern Moon" sequence and the marionette number are particularly amusing. To add to the merriment, MGM assembled a top-notch supporting cast which included Frank Morgan as Governor d'Annard, Elsa Lanchester as the Governor's wife, Cecilia Parker as Marietta's friend Julie, and Akim Tamiroff as Rudolpho, the gypsy king.

Check it out!
If you like this, you'll also like.....

The Girl of the Golden West (1938)

Dashing bandit Nelson Eddy didn't count on having his heart stolen by saloon keeper Jeanette MacDonald when he held up her stagecoach. He poses as an army officer in order to court her, but will he escape the trap laid by jealous sheriff Walter Pidgeon? Sprightly musical co-stars Buddy Ebsen, Leo Carrillo and Monty Wooley.

WARNER BROTHERS (1935)

SHIPMATES FOREVER

Singing sensation Dick Powell and dancer Ruby Keeler were a match made in musical heaven and they had great success in the early 1930s as an on-screen duo. In 1934, Warner Brothers teamed them up in *Flirtation Walk*, a light-hearted musical set at the West Point Military Academy. The studio reeled in a large profit on the picture and so they reteamed them to star in a similarly themed production - *Shipmates Foreve*r - this time set at the Annapolis Naval Academy. The publicity department even promoted the film with the line "Hats off to the Navy's Flirtation Walk!".

Dick Powell stars as Richard "Dick" Melville III, a popular New York nightclub singer who has no intention of joining the Navy and following in the footsteps of his father Admiral Melville (Lewis Stone). He is determined to lead his own life and singing is the career he chose. However, his father's claim that his only son is a coward, leads Richard to enter the Annapolis Naval Academy solely to prove to him that he has the brains to become an officer. Of course, while he is there he learns just what it means to be a "Navy man" and has a change of heart.

During the 1930s, there were a lot of movies made that dealt with life in military academies, it was as if the studios knew a war was looming in the distance. Along with *Navy Blue and Gold*, *Shipmates Forever* stands out as one of the best of these and, thanks to Frank Borzage's fine direction, the film has a lot of heart to it. For those who are especially fond of the Navy, you'll need to keep some handkerchiefs nearby for the closing scenes.

Shipmates Forever gives audiences a great behind-the-gates look at Annapolis with plenty of on-location footage. The movie also features a sweet romance between Ruby Keeler and Dick Powell and some catchy Harry Warren/Al Dubin numbers including the "Don't Give Up the Ship", "I'd Love to Take Orders from You", and "I'd Rather Listen to Your Eyes", but the best part of the film is Dick Powell's fine acting performance.

Powell was never given credit for being the talented actor that he was until he appeared in the noir *Murder, My Sweet* (1944) but, even in his early films, he was such a natural actor and always gave a winning performance. He is truly convincing as Dick Melville, a young man who seems torn between loyalty to his father, his best gal, and following his own dream. Even though he shuns his roommates at the Academy, they still look up to him as a classmate and eventually draw him into the comradery that was so much a part of life at Annapolis. These classmates are played by Ross Alexander and John Arledge (both from *Flirtation Walk*), Eddie Acuff, and Robert Light. Also in the cast is Dick Foran as a snooty upper-classman, Mary Treen, and James Flavin.

Shipmates Forever was re-leased in October 1935 and did very well at the box-office, cementing Dick Powell and Ruby Keeler's standing as one of the top on-screen couples at Warner Brothers studio at the time.

WARNER BROTHERS (1938)

The Adventures of ROBIN HOOD

"I'll never rest until every Saxon in this shire can stand up free men and strike a blow for Richard and England!"

Never has there been a more joyous swashbuckler filmed than Warner Brothers' *The Adventures of Robin Hood* (1938). The centuries old legend of the bold outlaw who robbed from the rich to give to the poor comes to life in this glorious adaptation which brims over with thrilling swordplay, sweet romance, a stellar cast, a thousand resplendent costumes, and a rousing orchestral score by Erich Wolfgang Korngold. Verily, the film serves up a right merry feast of entertainment.

No archer ever lived that could speed a gray goose shaft with such skill and cunning as Robin, nor has any actor embodied a character as well as Errol Flynn does in his portrayal of this lusty rogue.

The legends of Robin Hood date back to the 14th-century when tales of the famous outlaw were spread across the shires through ballads. Innumerable authors have passed the stories down in various tellings throughout the ages, but it is undoubtedly Howard Pyle's inspired adaptation of the legends in his 1883 masterpiece

FAMOUS AND FORGOTTEN FILMS

"The Merry Adventures of Robin Hood" that set the tone for this film.

Like the book, *The Adventures of Robin Hood* transports its audience to an England of yor; a time of grand pageantry, when knights roamed errant through virgin countryside in search of adventures and the world was bathed in the glow of medieval romance. It was also a time of oppression for serfs who were under the rule of scoundrelly noblemen, such as Sir Guy of Gisbourne.

Storybook thrills abound in Norman Reilly Raine and Seton Miller's script, which weave elements of romance, comedy, and adventure in its simple story of tyranny opposed and virtue triumphed. Robin Hood and his band of merry men, loyal to King Richard, set things right for England when the King's dastardly brother, the Norman Prince John, usurps the throne and wrenches tax money, yea, and the very blood, from the oppressed Saxons. The King's royal ward, Lady Marian, despises Robin Hood and his thieving ways until she sees the broken, destitute masses which he

cares for in the forest. Then her heart goes out towards him and his noble cause and she becomes the outlaw's ally, eventually saving him from the gallows.

James Cagney was originally cast as the archer in green tights when Warner Brothers began development on *Robin Hood* in 1935. The studio was slowly expanding its output to include adventure films and prestigious historical dramas in an effort to compete with its rival Metro-Goldwyn-Mayer and reach a broader audience.

After the success of Warner's *A Midsummer Night's Dream* (1935), costume designer Dwight Franklin suggested that the same formula could be translated well to another period piece, that of the tales of Robin Hood. Executive producer Hal Wallis decided to reunite most of the principle cast for this project, including Anita Louise as Lady Marian, Frank McHugh and Allen Jenkins as some of the merry men, and Hugh Herbert as Friar Tuck. Ho! but during the development stage James Cagney had one of his frequent rows with the studio and walked out on his contract, not returning for nearly two years.

FAMOUS AND FORGOTTEN FILMS 35

Since much time and money had already been invested in the story, Wallis decided to cast the studio's rising star, Errol Flynn, in the lead. The part of the charismatic Saxon knight was a glove-fit for this devilishly handsome actor who had a roguish air and an athletic knack for leaping over parapets.

Fate dealt a fortuitous hand with Cagney's departure, for Flynn's arrival precipitated a complete overhaul of the project. What resulted was a film which could not be more impeccably cast. Claude Rains cloaked himself in red as the villainous Prince John, an urbane schemer who finds the feather-capped archer's exploits wryly amusing. Basil Rathbone had a long career portraying villains and did a stellar performance as the wicked pirate Levasseur in *Captain Blood* in 1935. For this film he donned the garb of the egotistical Sir Guy of Gisbourne.

Lady Marian could not be envisioned more lovely than Olivia de Havilland, who had just launched her film career three years prior with her appearance as Hermia in *A Midsummer Night's Dream*. Once Errol Flynn was cast as Robin Hood there was no doubt that de Havilland would portray his "bold Norman beauty", since the two were such an ideal couple in *Captain Blood* and *The Charge of the Light Brigade*. They would go on to make six more films together.

Robin's rakish derring-do would be for naught without the aid he received from his motley band of merry men: Alan Hale had portrayed the bearish Little John in the 1922 Douglas Fairbanks version of Robin Hood, so it was a natural

FAMOUS AND FORGOTTEN FILMS

choice that he reprise the role for this film. Hale and Flynn were a right jolly team and over the course of their careers were united for 13 films. Patric Knowles was Robin's lyre-strumming comrade-in-arms Will Scarlett (a role originally intended for David Niven) and Eugene Palette portrayed the portly Friar Tuck.

Also in the cast was Herbert Mundin as cheerful Much, who casts a favorable eye on Marian's twittery lady-in-waiting Bess, portrayed by Una O'Connor. Ian Hunter made a noble King Richard, and Melville Cooper played the oafish Sheriff of Nottingham.

Shafts of sunlight streaming down through the leafy canopy of Sherwood Forest were captured in the splendor of three-strip Technicolor by the perceptive eyes of cinematographers Tony Gaudio and Sol Polito, who were utilizing the newly developed Technicolor cameras. This was a cumbersome and costly process, but it lent the film an unsurpassed richness in color. This beloved Sherwood of Robin's just happened to be Bidwell Park located in Chico, California. Never had England seen so much sunlight in one summer.

Director Michael Curtiz took over the scepter of command from William Keighley midway through production and deserves much credit for the sprightly pace of *The Adventures of Robin Hood*. He captured the grand-flourishing manner of silent day swashbucklers with their crowd-pleasing heroics and bold sword-play. Some of the sequences were even filmed "undercranked" which sped up the action on screen in silent-era fashion.

Errol Flynn was Douglas Fairbanks reincarnated with his broad-gestured displays of machismo. Stuntmen were used in some shots of the film, but many a daring-do was performed by Flynn himself who wanted it known that he did not shy away from physical feats.

The Adventures of Robin Hood was an enormous hit upon its initial release on May 14, 1938, with critics praising its sheer exuberance and audiences of all ages coming to take a pilgrimage to the land of medieval fancy. Robin's arrows soared through the air to land with a resounding ffffrupp! on the bullseye of entertainment. Warner Brothers gathered nearly $4 million into its purse and the film went on to win three of the four Oscars it was nominated for at the Academy Awards (losing the Best Picture award to *You Can't Take it With You*).

The Adventures of Robin Hood remains a favorite amongst cinephiles nearly eighty years since Robin made his heroic entrance into Sherwood Forest. It is still considered one of the best films of its type and possesses all of its initial zest and vitality, in no small part

FAMOUS AND FORGOTTEN FILMS

due to Errol Flynn's exuberant portrayal of Robin Hood. He shows us a character so supremely alive that to him all of life is a lark. What makes him so wonderful to behold is he lights the fire of life within the audience as well. Our cares disappear and we wonder why we take our petty problems with such seriousness when Robin could face death innumerable times without ever losing a feather in his cap.

Numerous remakes have been undertaken over the years but none have been able to capture the essence of Robin Hood without cynicism or postmodern mockery. This film was made with sublime innocence in a decade when righteousness and evil could be presented to the audience in simple black and white imagery without brushing virtues and sins together into murky grays. The cast and crew of Robin Hood set out to make the picture, not as a technical masterpiece, but purely for the aim of providing entertainment to the masses, and verily, this task was accomplished with thunderous success.

METRO-GOLDWYN-MAYER (1938)

LISTEN DARLING

For many years, Freddie Bartholomew was one of Metro-Goldwyn-Mayer's biggest box-office drawing child actors but, like most child stars, he found his popularity waning as he grew into adolescence. In 1938, he was no longer a wide-eyed aristocratic tyke, but had matured into a handsome - if a tad bit scrawny - teenager, just ripe enough in age to play a second-fiddle beau to the child actor who would succeed him as star of the studio - Judy Garland - in the family melodrama *Listen, Darling*.

Judy Garland had been signed to a MGM contract in 1935 and had quickly become such a favorite with audiences across the country that within three short years the studio was already preparing an adaptation of Frank L. Baum's "The Wizard of Oz" to be a starring vehicle for their newfound talent.

Her characters were often shy, giggly, awkward little girls, but they were strangely appealing. Judy had a way of brightening up the screen the moment she walked into a scene and, when she opened her mouth to sing, that powerful voice of hers would transfix audiences. Her singing was very mature and heart-felt for one so young.

FAMOUS AND FORGOTTEN FILMS

Judy had starred in only a handful of roles (her most recent being opposite Mickey Rooney in *Love Finds Andy Hardy*) when she was cast in *Listen, Darling*, a light-hearted melodrama aimed towards juvenile audiences. Today, it is remembered primarily for her performance of the song "Zing! Went the Strings of my Heart" (which Judy kept in her stage repertoire until her final show some thirty years later) but the film itself has many endearing qualities. It is quite touching and often humorous.

Judy stars as young Pinkie Wingate who, with her pal Buzz (Freddie), will stop at nothing - including kidnapping - to keep her mother (Mary Astor) from entering a loveless marriage with the town's pompous banker (Gene Lockhart). Together they stow mother and baby brother into the old family trailer and head onto the open road to look for a handsome man who could whisk her mother off her feet. They think it will be a bumpy road to love but their mother quickly catches the eye of two suitors (Walter Pidgeon and Alan Hale), who, in Pinky's eyes, are both preferable to the banker.

Freddie Bartholomew and Judy Garland make a winning team of cupids but, since they were at opposite arcs in their careers, this would be their only screen pairing. Bartholomew confessed that he had a crush on Judy during the making of the movie but she only looked upon him as a younger brother, being a whole two years older than he.

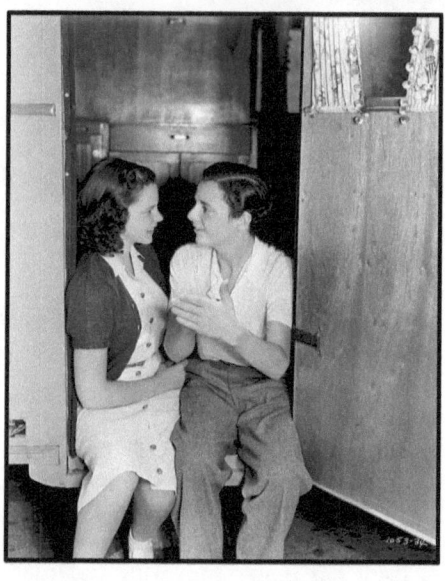

Listen, Darling is a sweet film and features that unabashed sentimentality which only MGM could capture on film so well. I especially enjoy it because of the fond memories I associate with the movie. One beautiful Saturday morning, my father, sister, and I were returning home from a camping trip at the lakeside town of Geneva, Ohio, when we stopped at a small library and found a mother-load of classic movies on VHS tape in their collection.... one of which was *Listen, Darling*. On most Saturday nights we watch MGM musicals or Walt Disney films, so we saw *Listen, Darling* that very evening to cap off that wonderful day and zing! went the strings of my heart.... the film drew me in completely. Its fun camping theme and the spot-on performances from all the principal players made it a delight to watch and it has always remained a favorite.

NUGGET REVIEWS

"There's gold in them thar films!"

There certainly is... and to help our readers sift through all the glittery golden gems that can be found throughout the vast classic filmdom, old Pete the prospector is here to give us his "caret" ratings.

With the Nugget Reviews he will give you a little synopsis and some quick comments about the flick and hopefully you will discover a hidden golden nugget whilst panning the flowing streams of movie history.

Ol' Pete knows pure gold when he sees it, so if he tells you it's a spud, it's a spud. You better believe it!

CANYON PASSAGE (1946) 14k

A mule train owner is torn between his love for two women and his loyalty to his best friend, a shifty gambler. Dana Andrews, Susan Hayward, Brian Donlevy, Ward Bond. Universal Pictures. Directed by Jacques Tourneur.

That Ward Bond. He can be a real good guy when he wants to and a real bad guy when it is called for. In *Canyon Passage* he was a brute. Dana Andrews has his deadpan face in place but managed to convey enough emotion to make you root for him to get his gal. Susan Hayward was looking pretty but the real star of the show was Umpqua National Forest which was looking simply stunning thanks to Edward Cronjager's brilliant Technicolor cinematography. An engrossing - and highly underrated - western.

The Rating System:

24 Carat: This is glistening gold folks. You won't find any finer. Either the movie's entertainment is of such a high caliber that it earns this rating, or else the quality of the film deserves this rank.

18 Carat: A grand find! It may not be the among the golden mother-load but it has many fine qualities and deserves to be glittering in the spotlight.

14 Carat: Standard fare. These are movies that are worth seeing once in a while, or if you have a personal taste for them. Your favorites can run along here. Mine does.

Electroplated Gold: This looks good from the title and the back of the DVD case but once you watch it you know you've been had. Big time.

Fool's Gold: If you spent your time watching this then yer just as big a jackass as Pete's mule Harry.

LONDON FILMS (1939)

THE FOUR FEATHERS

Every generation of the Favershams have had a military hero, but even as a boy Harry Faversham thought war futile and did not wish to follow in his illustrious family's footsteps. As his father explained to a comrade, *"I send him to the best army school in England, spend half my time telling him about his famous ancestors and what do you think? I found him this morning reading poetry.... Shelley of all people!"*

As Harry (John Clements) matured, his viewpoint of war did not alter but, not wishing to displease his father, he enters the British Army. However, while saying goodbye to his fiancee Ethne (June Duprez), he reconsiders his decision and on the eve of the day his company is to leave to join Kitchener's army in Sudan, he resigns his commission. Harry feels that his future with Ethne and living a peaceful life in England is more important than fighting a hopeless battle in the desert.

"The futility of this idiotic Egyptian adventure and the madness of it all, the ghastly waste of time that we can never have again!"

His commanding officer is very displeased with him, as are his three boyhood friends who each send him a white feather, a symbol of cowardice. This does not affect him so much as does hearing his sweetheart agree with them:

"You were not born free Harry, and nor was I. We were born into a tradition, a code which we must obey even if we do not believe in it.....and we must obey because the pride and happiness of everyone around us depends upon our obedience."

Filled with angry passion, he plucks off a white feather from her fan and adds them to the group, making four feathers. He secretly vows to prove his courage to Ethne, his companions ...and himself. The way he goes about this is above and beyond the call of duty. This is where the romance ends and the adventure begins.

During the late 1930s many British Imperialism-themed adventure spectacles were released, but Alexander Korda's *The Four Feathers* (1939) is by far the best Filmed on location in the Middle East in glorious Technicolor, we follow Harry on various escapades throughout Egypt, climaxing in a battle at Obdurman, before we return to England for the "showdown". For a film that is not even two full hours in length, it manages to squeeze in quite a bit of story and a lot of excitement, as well as a tender sub-romance involving Captain John Durrance (Ralph Richardson), one of Harry's friends, and Ethne.

The beloved character actor C. Aubrey Smith plays one of his usual bombastic gentleman roles, that of Ethne's father, a retired general who likes to recount a tale of his bravery in battle using the fruit and nuts from the dinner table.

"Now the Crimean...... war was war in those days, and men were men!"

With spectacular filming, breathtaking color, a sweeping Miklos Rozsa score, thrilling battle scenes (that have cropped up again as clips in many other films), and excellent cast performances, *The Four Feathers* is a real gem. The story is not a new one, however.

"The Four Feathers" was originally a novel written by A.E.W. Mason in 1902 and its first screen-telling was made in 1915. It was remade in 1929 with the dashing Richard Arlen, Fay Wray, Clive Brook, and William Powell.

After the blockbuster Korda version, it was made yet again in 1955 by RKO (inferiorly) as *Storm Over the Nile* starring Anthony Steele, Lawrence Harvey, and Ian Carmichael. Ah, but who wants to stop at four versions? In 1977, *The Four Feathers* was aired as a made-for-TV film starring Beau Bridges, Robert Powell, Jane Seymour and Simon Ward. More recently, in 2002, it was filmed yet again with Heath Ledger, Wes Bentley, and Kate Hudson in the starring roles.

Unless you have a passion for comparison, don't even bother with these other versions because to this day, Korda's 1939 *The Four Feathers* remains the crown-jewel of them all.

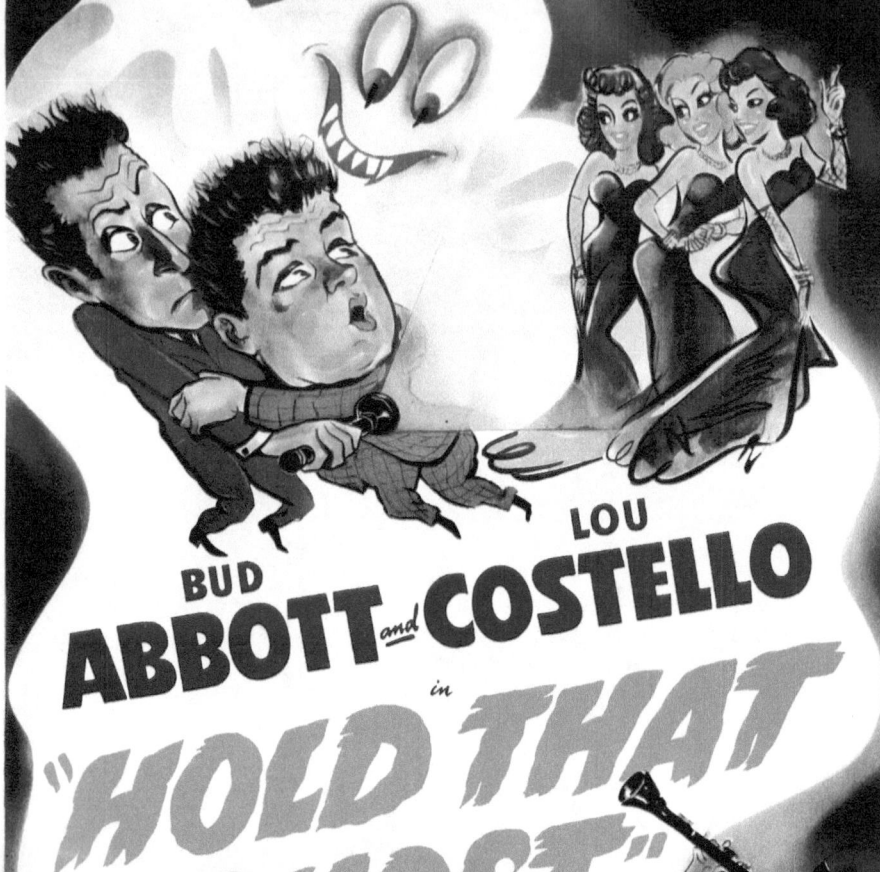

UNIVERSAL PICTURES (1940)

Hold That Ghost

Gas station attendants Chuck (Bud Abbott) and Ferdie (Lou Costello) happen to be present when gangster Moose Matson (William Davidson) is shot by the police during a car chase. His last will and testament leave all that he owns to those who are present at his death, hence the boys inherit Moose's fortune which happens to be a rundown roadhouse in the outskirts of town. While checking out the property they inherited, they get stranded there on a stormy night with an odd conglomerate of travelers from the cab they were sharing. Moose's old cronies believe that Matson hid a fortune in the roadhouse and so they attempt to frighten Chuck and Ferdie and the other guests away from the house so they can search for the loot.

Hold That Ghost was the fourth of 35 films that the comedy team of Abbott and Costello made during the 1940s and 1950s and it ranks as one of their best. It has all the spooktacular features you would want to see in a haunted house comedy plus the added bonus of a great cast.

Scream-queen Evelyn Ankers joins the duo as one of the guests at the roadhouse, as does Richard Carlson and slapschtick sensation Joan Davis. Marc Lawrence, one of the most famous film gangsters of the era, plays Charlie Smith who turns up stiff. Also making

appearances are Shemp Howard, Mischa Auer, Bobby Barber (who later played Stinky on *The Abbott and Costello Show*), and Ted Lewis and the Andrews Sisters.

Abbott and Costello never needed any help from supporting players to add to their comedic fun, but *Hold That Ghost* is a real treat because of the presence of Joan Davis. This marvelous comedienne made a number of films as a leading star but her best performances were in films where she had a supporting role. In *Hold That Ghost*, she plays a fellow passenger who is stranded at the inn. Ferdie (Costello) finds her annoying and it is in the scenes where the two banter that most of the humor is to be found. They also share one of the best comedic dance scenes put on film. Davis should have reteamed with Costello in their second mystery-comedy *Who Done It?* (1942) but instead that film featured Mary Wickes.

"You boys ready to leave?"
- Joan Davis

"I was ready to leave when he put the key in the front door!" - Lou Costello

From its wonderful animated opening credits to its peppy closing number ("Aurora" sung by the Andrews Sisters), *Hold That Ghost* never lets up on the laughs. Many of the routines that Abbott and Costello would perform in this film, such as the moving candle trick, were later reused in future films and television episodes.

The duo had skyrocketed to stardom after their first picture *Buck Privates* was released just a year earlier and it is amazing how quickly they had to be able to come up with comedy routines thereafter. Universal Studios had screenwriters penning scripts for them and the boys were busy filming month after month. In 1941 alone, four Abbott and Costello movies were released.

Hold that Ghost, originally titled *Oh, Charlie!*, was slated to be released right after *Buck Privates* but when that film became a blockbuster hit for Universal, the studio decided to put *Oh, Charlie!* on the shelf to give them time to make another service comedy in the vein of *Buck Privates*. *In the Navy* was quickly put into production and released right after completion. Since the Andrews Sisters had appeared in both films, it was decided that they would make a great addition to *Hold That Ghost* as well, so Abbott and Costello were brought back to the studio to film a

new opening and closing that featured the singing threesome.

In spite of the popularity of both *Hold That Ghost* and *Who Done It?*, Abbott and Costello did not return to the mystery/horror genre until 1948 when they made *Abbott and Costello Meet Frankenstein*, which not only brought them back to the top of the box-office charts but launched a series of similarly themed monster comedies.... unfortunately, none of which were as good as this gem.

FAMOUS AND FORGOTTEN FILMS

UNIVERSAL PICTURES (1941)

"Even a man who is pure in heart and says his prayers at night, may become a wolf when the wolf bane blooms and the autumn moon is bright"

Larry Talbot may not have been a man "pure in heart" but he was a man who certainly didn't expect to be turned into a howling beast when the wolf bane bloomed. Who does for that matter? Poor guy. He was just a luckless lump who happened to be in the wrong place at the wrong time.

After 18 years spent abroad in America, Larry Talbot returns to his ancestral home in Llanwelly, Wales, only to find that a dangerous date with destiny awaits him.

While escorting his sweetheart, the lovely Evelyn Ankers, through a gypsy encampment, he hears the scream of her friend Jenny in the woods, runs to rescue her from a wolf....and gets bitten in the process!

With his newly purchased silver handled wolf-carved cane, he had bludgeoned the wolf to death during the struggle. But lo! the next morning he finds his wound has disappeared and the police are questioning him about the death of Bela (played by the inimitable legend of horror, Bela Lugosi)..... the gypsy he had supposedly mistaken for a wolf. To make matters worse, Bela's mother (Maria Ospenskaya) tells Larry that having now been bitten, he will become a wolf as well. But,  being our everyday all-American disbelieving film hero, he promptly disregards the wise old gypsy's warning and the protective charm she gives him, a foolish act that leads him straight into danger. Oh dear, won't these guys ever learn?

Filming on *The Wolf Man* began just before Halloween 1941. It was completed and released in December and went on to become one of the top grossing pictures of the year.

Dick Foran, a popular B-film and cowboy star, was originally intended for the role of Larry Talbot but was replaced one week prior to filming. A good thing too, for Lon Chaney Jr. was very fond and proud of the Wolf Man character and made a career of playing him. He welcomed the opportunity of starring in the many sequels such as *Frankenstein Meets the Wolf Man*, *House of Frankenstein*, *House of Dracula* and the really horrifying classic, *Abbott and Costello Meet Frankenstein*.

When Lon Chaney Jr., the son of the famous "Man of a Thousands Faces" Lon Chaney Sr, was offered the lead role in *The Wolf Man*, he was not yet known for being a horror film actor. He had enjoyed success on stage in Steinbeck's "Of Mice and Men" and had appeared in the film adaptation in 1939. Chaney was up for the lead in Universal's remake of *The Phantom of the Opera* in 1940, but alas..it was his Wolf Man father, Claude Rains who won that choice part. Instead, Chaney starred in *Man Made Monster* (1941) and director George Waggner was so pleased with his performance that he quickly plopped him into his next picture, *The Wolf Man*. A legendary horror icon was born!

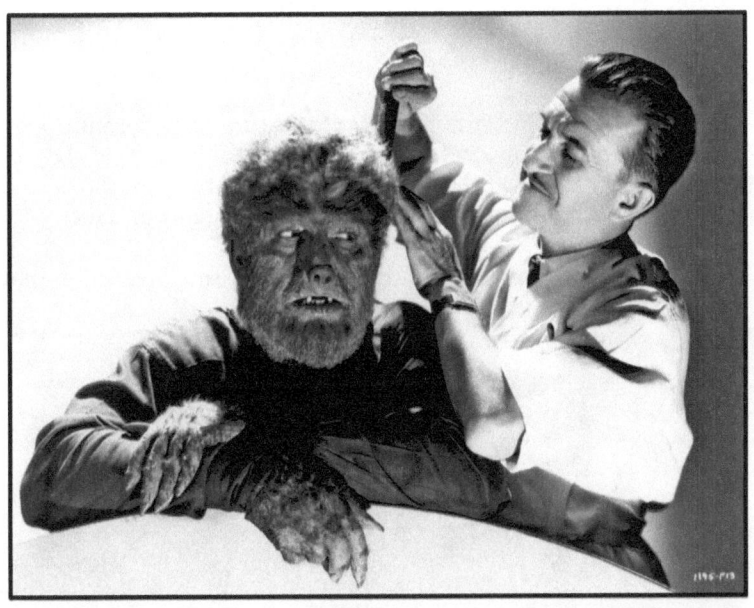

Although he played an innocent victim of circumstances on screen, off-screen Chaney was quite a hooligan. He had vandalized studio property one day while drunk and, as punishment, Waggner assigned his star dressing room to Ankers. After spending grueling hours having makeup artist Jack Pierce apply yak hair and a rubber schnozz to him every morning, and then wait another 45 minutes after shooting to have it removed, Chaney was upset at having his dressing room taken. He had a fondness for playing practical jokes and Ankers quickly became the prime recipient of them. He enjoyed sneaking up on her in full makeup and scaring her. One incident, however, was not Chaney's fault....a 600 pound bear which was used in an eliminated sequence, escaped one afternoon from its trainer and chased Ms. Ankers up a ladder.

Evelyn Ankers, who played Larry's gal Gwenn Conliffe in the film, was known as the "Scream Queen" of the 1940s and was very busy that decade making horror films such as *The Ghost of Frankenstein*, *Son of Dracula*, and *The Invisible Man's Revenge*. She also starred in a couple entries in the popular Universal Sherlock Holmes film series: *The Pearl of Death* and *Sherlock Holmes and the Voice of Terror*.

The Wolf Man was not the first film to feature hairy lycanthropes. Six years earlier Universal had made *The Werewolf of London* starring Henry Hull as a botanist who receives that notorious wolf bite while hunting for a rare flower in the mountains of Tibet.

This film did not gross much at the box-office, so Universal so they

FAMOUS AND FORGOTTEN FILMS

gave it another try and in 1941 the viewing public was much more gullible and embraced *The Wolf Man*. It was released just days after the attack on Pearl Harbor so it proved to be escapism at its finest. To this day it remains a classic and justly so; with its smothering foggy atmosphere, superb supporting cast (including Claude Rains, Ralph Bellamy, Warren William, and Patric Knowles), and excellent set design, it leaves a lasting impression. So much so that when the autumn moon is bright, our thoughts naturally turn to the Wolf Man of the night.

Check it out!
If you like this, you'll also like.....

The Undying Monster (1942)

Surviving members of an aristocratic English family are threatened by a legendary monster who strikes when the moon is full. James Ellison and Heather Angel star in this atmospheric mystery from director John Brahm.

METRO-GOLDWYN-MAYER (1943)

Above Suspicion

"My love is like a red, red rose...."

MGM journeys into the realm of espionage with *Above Suspicion* (1943), a witty jaunt into spy-laden pre-World War II Europe.

Fred MacMurray plays Richard Myles, an Oxford college professor, who is happily ready to embark on a Continental honeymoon with his bride Frances (Joan Crawford). Before they depart however, a former colleague of his, now with the foreign office, asks the couple if they would do a favor to him and jolly ol' England by inquiring into the whereabouts of a scientist who has disappeared within the confines of the Fuhrer's

Vaterland. He holds the secret plans to the Nazi's latest diabolical invention - underwater magnetic mines. As honeymooners they would be considered above suspicion and could look into the matter discreetly. Or so they are told. Ach du lieber! ... before they can utter "uberraschung" they are caught up in a web of intrigue that leads them from Paris to the pine-laden Alpine forests of Innsbruck.

Above Suspicion was based on the novel by Helen MacInnes and is an easy-to-follow and briskly paced thriller with some rattling good moments of excitement. Its purely escapist plot is given credibility through its deft handling by director Richard Thorpe (*Night Must Fall*, *Ivanhoe*) and its stellar cast. The film plays out along the lines of *Desperate Journey* with grand morale-boosting elements but very little plausibility..... but perhaps that's what makes both of these pictures so entertaining. *Above Suspicion* was released at the height of World War II, a time when so many American and British citizens were eager to make an active contribution to corking up the war for good.

"Darling, the less you know, or appear to know, the better"

At one time or another we're all drawn in by the allure of being a spy; deciphering codes, staking out suspicious bookshop fronts, wearing disguises, hiding out in secluded chalets and, of course, capturing public enemies. Richard and Frances are no different, and Frances is especially thrilled to help the British secret service but, unlike his wife, Richard realizes the danger ahead. En route, our American heroes stumble upon cryptic clues, all the while being spied on with peering abnormality by dubious faces and sundry characters. Their only key to unmasking friends from foes lies within the lyrics to an eighteenth century melody by Robert Burns.

In addition to our leading cast, *Above Suspicion* features some excellent character support from Basil Rathbone, Felix Bressart, Reginald Owen, Richard Ainley, Bruce Lester and Sara Haden. Conrad Veidt is especially appealing in his role as Herr Seidel, one of the Brit's loyal allies within Germany. Veidt was often pigeonholed as villains and it is a pleasant change of face to see him play this underground hero. Veidt died of a massive stroke shortly after filming commenced and Hollywood lost one of its most talented actors because of his passing. His entertaining dance floor sequence is a highlight of the film.

Fred MacMurray was making a departure from his recent Claudette Colbert comedy teamings to take a dramatic turn and this role suits him quite well. Incidentally, Colbert would have made an excellent Frances had Crawford declined the part.

Joan Crawford had been loyal to Metro-Goldwyn-Mayer since they gave her her start in 1925. She made seventeen films with the studio but by the early 1940s her star-status was beginning to wane and fresh faces like Lana Turner, Hedy Lamarr, and Greer Garson were receiving all of the choice scripts. Eager to showcase her acting ability, Crawford accepted a lower salary and switched to the less prestigious Warner Brothers studio after the completion of *Above Suspicion*. Within one year she was up for the Academy Award for Best Actress for her portrayal in *Mildred Pierce*.

Within *Above Suspicion* are hidden elements of Hitchcock-like suspense, featuring a labyrinth of twists and turns, car chases, and an assassination attempt at an opera, a scene taken right out of *The Man Who Knew Too Much* (1934). Overall, the film is like a tasty strudel filled with chunks of drama, comedy and action, all enfolded within thin layers of plot to make up a taut 90-minute thriller.

METRO-GOLDWYN-MAYER (1943)

ASSIGNMENT IN BRITTANY

"Every second throbs with suspense and danger!"

For once, those exclamatory theatrical heralds were right: *Assignment in Brittany* is packed to the brim with non-stop adventure. There is so much fast-paced excitement that if you do not have your ears pricked up and your eyes glued to the screen, you may lose some of the plot line.

French heart-throb Jean-Pierre Aumont plays Pierre Matard, a captain in the Free French forces, who is sent to a small village in France disguised as Bertrand Corlay (also Aumont), a suspected Nazi collaborator. Since Pierre bears such a striking resemblance to this man, his task is to weasel out information about the location of a U-Boat base that the British believe is in the vicinity. For the audiences benefit, he accomplishes this mission in one and one-half hours filled with exciting moments of danger.

Like many films that were made in the midst of the war, the brutality of war is not softened to appeal to audience tastes. In one scene, many of the friends that Aumont's character comes to know are executed in front of his eyes. The Nazis are portrayed as the fiendish brutes that they were. But there are tender moments as well. All good resistance fighters end up falling in love while on their missions and Captain Pierre has his moment of romance when his heart melts for the fiancee of his look-a-like Bertrand: Anne Pinot, portrayed by Susan Peters.

Assignment in Brittany (1943) marked the debut of Jean-Pierre Aumont, who had arrived in Hollywood just a year earlier and could barely speak English. It was stage actress Katharine Cornell who discovered the handsome Jean Gabin-esque actor and cast him in her play "Rose Burke". Shortly after he was signed to an MGM contract and made this film and another war drama, *The Cross of Lorraine*, that same year. Aumont himself had earned the Legion of Honor and Croix de Guerre medals for his service in North Africa with the Free French Forces from 1939-1940. While in Hollywood, he helped raise funds for the Resistance and returned to fight in 1944.

Also making her American debut was Swedish actress Signe Hasso. She made a number of excellent war films, usually playing a heroine but, in this film, she is quite the vixen.

Like most MGM pictures, the production values on *Assignment in Brittany* are top-notch with great sets by Cedric Gibbons and Edwin Willis, costumes by Gile Steele, music by Lennie Hayton, and excellent cinematography by Charles Rosher *(Annie Get Your Gun)*. The script to the film was based on a Helen MacInnes novel that was serialized in 1942 in "The Saturday Evening Post". MacInnes was a prolific author of espionage novels and, in 1943, MGM had turned another one of her books into a box-office hit - *Above Suspicion*.

Assignment in Brittany has the usual elements that you would hope to find in an espionage film: suspicious double-face characters, secret codes, danger behind every corner, plenty of Gestapo agents, and the classic escape-in-disguise (this time taking place within a church in France).

The film's director, Jack Conway, was a veteran of silent films and numerous MGM "A" pictures *(A Tale of Two Cities, Libeled Lady, Boom Town, The Hucksters)*. He was an excellent director and was capable of handling comedies, dramas, and action films with equal ease. The final scene of the destruction of the U-boat base is especially well-filmed and really caps off the picture with a bang.

The movie boasts a strong supporting cast of MGM stock actors such as Margaret Wycherly, Richard Whorf, Reginald Owen, Alan Napier, Miles Mander, and John Emery. Also, a young Darryl Hickman is given a meaty role as a little French freedom fighter.

Desperate Journey (1942)

During WWII, five American pilots (including Errol Flynn and Ronald Reagan) are shot down over Germany and must use all of their cunning and willpower to try to escape to safety in the Netherlands. Spirited WWII drum-beater from Warners co-stars Raymond Massey, Arthur Kennedy, Alan Hale, Ronald Sinclair, Sig Ruman.

LES FILMS RICHEBÉ (1943)

Les Anges du Péché

"If you hear God's word joining you to another, listen to no other words - they are merely its echo."

- St. Catherine of Siena

Director Robert Bresson's first feature film, the underrated gem *Les Anges du Péché* aka *Angels of Sin*, explores the indistinguishable line between will and chance and the effect people have in determining each other's destinies, a theme that resonated throughout Bresson's later works (*The Diary of a Country Priest, A Man Escaped*).

The story follows Sœur Anne-Marie (Renée Faure) a young bourgeois-born novice at a Dominican convent who is convinced that she was sent by God to save the soul of Sœur Thérèse (Jany Holt), an impenitent murderess who joins the order to seek shelter from the police.

Father Bruckberger, an acquaintance of Bresson's, had suggested he read "The Dominicans of the Prisons" by Father Lelong and proposed a film about the Sisters of Bethany in France, an order of nuns devoted to working with female ex-convicts. The order, founded in 1866, gives these women the opportunity to overcome the sins that led them to become criminals. Some choose to remain at the convent and become nuns while others venture on to begin a new life.

Although Bresson was ignorant of Bethany, he was intrigued by the premise and developed an engrossing scenario around it that weaves in key elements that Bresson would return to in every subsequent film he made. He was particularly fascinated with the theme of two lives coming together and forging a preordained course, one which ends in redemption for both.

While Sœur Anne-Marie is the main character in *Les Anges du Péché* and dominates the majority of the scenes, her presence is merely a clever red-herring from Bresson for the film is truly about Sœur Thérèse. It is her soul's redemption that is the driving force of the picture and all the events that take place at the abbey from the day of her arrival act as stepping stones of grace leading up to her redemption.

In one scene, the nuns gather for a ceremony where each sister receives a maxim, a randomly chosen quote, that will become their motto for the year. These maxims miraculously suit the personality of each sister. St. Catherine's quote about hearing "God's word joining you to another" is handed to Anne-Marie and has a particularly awe-inspiring effect upon her because she felt an invisible Hand drawing her towards the prison, specifically towards Thérèse, ever since she arrived at the convent.

Evidently, Sœur Anne-Marie's heavenly calling to save such a lost lamb as Thérèse was conceived before she even meets her, but she

ultimately succeeds in her task only when she comes to recognize her own failures and humble herself. Her optimistic determination to accomplishing what she considers God's will, and her pride in her divine vocation, others perceive merely as sinful arrogance. She recognizes this when she subjects herself to "sisterly correction" and goes cell to cell asking each sister "How do you value me?". She finds that they see her as being selfish, ambitious, and showing no understanding of others. The nuns do not recognize her irrepressible fervor as being a sign of deeper spirituality. Only Thérèse refuses to rebuke her.

Thérèse considers herself dead to sin. She is unrepentant. She has accomplished her murderous act of revenge towards the man who let her be wrongfully incarcerated and is now the most obedient nun at the convent, finding life there preferable - if not dissimilar - to life imprisonment. Yet, she is impatient with Anne-Marie's chastenings and is relieved when the prioress sends Anne-Marie away from the convent, not realizing that even that act is simply another step leading her towards her preordained destiny - the path of redemption.

Robert Bresson would later favor a sparse naturalistic approach to filming, using a minimum amount of background music, little dialogue, and completely renouncing professional actors. *Les Anges du Péché* and *Les Dames du Bois de Boulogne* (1945) were the only two films he made with professional actors, a choice which he strangely regretted. Bresson, who in his "Notes" cautioned himself against drawing "tears from the public with the tears of your models" failed to realize that naturalism can only entertain to a point. Its novelty wears off and the audience yearns to see emotions and characterizations that professional actors demonstrate best.

The performances of Renée Faure, Jany Holt, and Louise Sylvie (as La Prieure) are expressive and beautiful and add depth to the characters in such a subtle way that non-professional actors could not have accomplished. Holt, in particular, gives a touching understated performance while Faure is convincingly innocent and saintlike.

A strong supporting cast (Mila Parély, Silvia Monfort, Louis Seigner), gorgeous cinematography by Philippe Agostini, and a powerful score by Jean-Jacques Grünenwald add up to making this an impressive directorial debut from Bresson and a true French cinema classic.

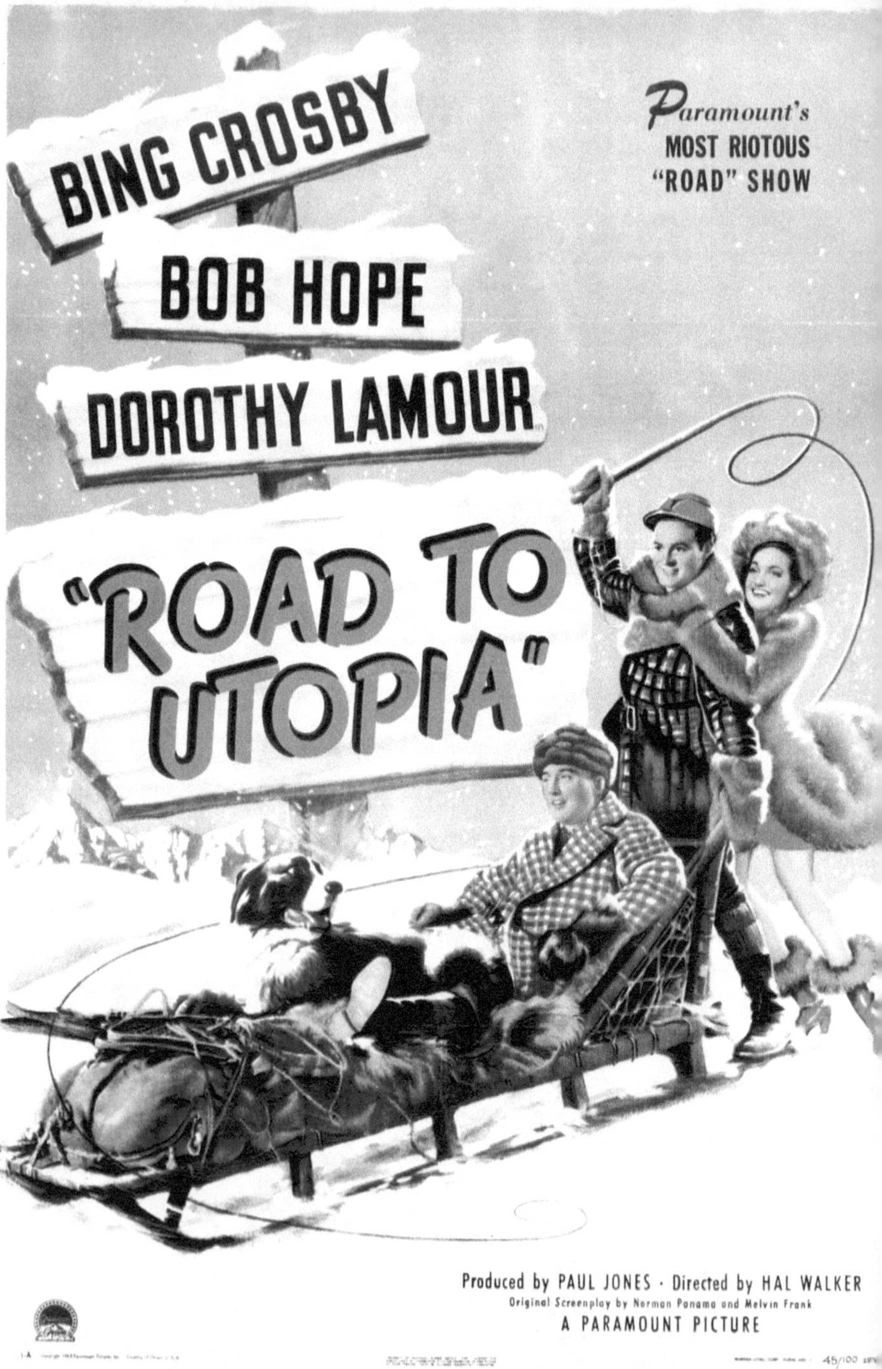

BING CROSBY
BOB HOPE
DOROTHY LAMOUR
Paramount's
MOST RIOTOUS
"ROAD" SHOW
"ROAD TO UTOPIA"
Produced by PAUL JONES · Directed by HAL WALKER
Original Screenplay by Norman Panama and Melvin Frank
A PARAMOUNT PICTURE

PARAMOUNT PICTURES (1945)

THE ROAD TO UTOPIA

Bob Hope and Bing Crosby are on the road once again in the 1945 comedy classic *Road to Utopia*, this time heading out to Alaska during the Klondike gold rush at the turn of the century. Hope and Crosby play a couple of down-in-their-luck vaude-villians named Chester and Duke who find a map to a gold mine, a map initially stolen by Sperry and McGurk, two murderous thugs who are hot on the two-some's trail to retrieve the map. En route to Alaska, Chester and Duke lose their money and stow away on a steamer. After they are caught, they assume the identities of Sperry and McGurk in order to disembark un-

Songs:
"Welcome To My Dream"
"Would You"
"Personality"
"It's Anybody's Spring"
"Put It There Pal"

observed. This is when the film really gets fun watching the cowardly Chester and mild-mannered Duke swagger and snarl as they masquerade as tough guys.

"I'll have a lemonade," Chester barks at the bartender and then, realizing he was supposed to be Sperry, adds with a growl "....*in a dirty glass!*"

Also on the trail of the map to the gold mine is the curvaceous Sal (Dorothy Lamour), whose father was murdered for the map. Ace Larson (Douglas Dumbrille) and his gal Kate (Hillary Brooke) claim they will help her retrieve it but they too are after it for themselves. We never do get to see this elusive gold mine but the fun of the chase for the map makes up the best parts of the picture.

Road to Utopia was the fourth film in the Road Pictures series and it ranks as one of their most hilarious. Crosby and Hope are clearly having a ball and their verbal sparring is furious and fun. Their dialogue is delivered so off the cuff that one wonders how much of it was written in the script and how much was impromptu. The words that were written on paper earned screenwriters Melvin Frank and Norman Panama an Academy Award nomination for Best Original Screenplay.

"Am I dead?" - Chester

"I can't tell, you always look that way." - Duke

Like many of the *Road* pictures, the "fourth wall" is often broken with Bob Hope making sly glances and remarks to the audience. This one also features humorous breaks from Robert Benchley who comments on the silliness of the script.

Silliness it indeed is, but this is what makes the film so amusing. Hope and Crosby deliver their lines and then add some personal comments and a little playful bickering before going back to playing their parts. Plus, der Bingel takes time to sing a few songs including the memorable "Welcome to My Dreams". Johnny Burke and Jimmy Van Heusen penned the songs for the film and Dorothy Lamour's sizzling rendition of "Personality" hit #1 on the music charts that year.

Hope and Crosby would return to the sweltering climates of the other Road pictures in *Road to Rio* (1947) but for wintertime fun you can't beat this Alaskan outing with the twosome.

LENFILM STUDIOS (1947)

CINDERELLA

Classic foreign films are often presented as being moody atmospheric dramas or visual voyages into surrealism, but anyone who has enjoyed a classic Russian film knows how beautiful and how colorful their films truly were. They definitely did not follow the brooding European noir-style trend of the 1940s and 1950s.

Cinderella, aka *Zolushka*, is a prime example of Russia's imaginative styling. This family film combines live-action with some marvelous stop-motion animation to create a beautiful presentation of the traditional fairy tale. It is a delightful film filled with ingenuous characters who wear their emotions on their sleeves.

Zolushka was released by Lenfilms in 1947 and follows the traditional Cinderella fable quite closely with poor little Zolushka slaving away in the country cottage where she resides with her stepmother and her two step-sisters, patiently waiting for the day when she will be freed from them. Unlike the original story, Cinderella now has a father.... the Royal Forester. Why does this father let his daughter be a servant to his second wife and his two step-daughters? Because, like in many Russian films, men who are married to nagging wives are portrayed as broken men, accepting of their situation and not willing to speak against their wives. It is certainly a far cry from the portrayal of outspoken Russian men that we are shown in American films. One day, the fairy Godmother senses the child's desire to glimpse the royal ball taking place that evening, and magically bedecks Zolushka in garments fit for a princess. She sends her along the way in a royal carriage with the stern warning that she leave the ball before the strike of midnight, that bewitched hour when her garments will return to tatters.

Zolushka is at the ball but a few hours when she falls in love with a young prince, a noble lad who returns her affection. Together they are transported to the Land of Magic, courtesy of the court magician, where Cinderella realizes the kind of happiness that she missed all the years before. It is at that inopportune moment that the clock strikes midnight. Cinderella flees from the palace in the nick of time, only to lose her glass slipper in her flight. This slipper becomes the sole clue for the Prince to use when he seeks out the identity of the unknown beauty who stepped into his life.

In Zolushka, all of the characters speak honestly and openly of their feelings toward each other (good or bad) and this unabashed candor is so very refreshing to watch. We tend to mask our feelings so often, or feel ashamed of expressing our true feelings to others, so it is truly wonderful to see characters be as frank as we, ourselves, would like to be.... and should be.

Yanina Zhejmo, who portrays Zolushka, was a popular actress in the 1940s, combining the adorable facial features of Sonja Henie with the singing voice of Ilona Massey. She perfectly captured the humble qualities of Cinderella as well as her childlike nature, which is surprising considering she was 38-years old at the time of filming. Zhejmo made a number of films throughout the 1930s and 1940s, but, unfortunately, most of these are not available stateside. Her final feature film was voicing the titular character in *The Snow Queen* (1957), one of Russia's most beloved animated classics.

Aleksey Konsovskiy, who plays the Prince,

was also in his mid-thirties. While he looks like a sissy from outward appearances, this Prince is actually quite a man... being more noble in nature than most young men seen in modern films. Both Konsovskiy and Zhejmo perform two lovely operetta-like songs.

One of the most entertaining characters in Zolushka is the King, played by Erast Garin. This eccentric king has a very low patience level and when he becomes exasperated he throws off his wig and declares he is going to join a monastery (!). Outdoing his zaniness is the Minister of Dance, who naturally serves no other position but to prance around the court and amuse the king.

Characters like these, added to the fantasy animation-style settings, clearly imply that *Cinderella* was meant for children to enjoy. However, the film is so engaging that you need not be a child, or watch it with a child, to enjoy it. It stands as an admirable example of classic Russian cinema: imaginative, humorous, and highly entertaining.

20th CENTURY FOX (1947)

The Ghost and Mrs. Muir

"Haunted.....how perfectly fascinating!"

Recently widowed Lucy Muir desires to start a new life. In pursuit of this, she has left her London lodgings, and her in-laws, to come to Whitecliff-by-the-sea with her daughter and loyal housemaid. There, situated atop a lovely coastal cliff, she finds her ideal home....Gull Cottage. It is up for rent.

"And priced at only 54 pounds per week. That's very inexpensive for a furnished house."

Strong-minded Lucy will not even let the thought of a ghost scare her away from Gull Cottage. The idea of returning to London and the life she led before is not a choice she wants to consider. Even the gruff and determined Captain Daniel Gregg - the apparition she comes to

FAMOUS AND FORGOTTEN FILMS

meet there one dark and stormy night - yields to her wish to remain at his beloved home.

He had been frightening away, with his boyish pranks, all prospective tenants to Gull Cottage for the last several years and the fact that Mrs. Muir chooses to stay in spite of knowing he haunts the house wins her his admiration.

During their coming year together, a gentle love blossoms between this ghost of a roguish sea captain and the spirited Victorian widow. She comes to see Captain Gregg not only as a dear friend but as an anchor and a pillar of support. Their relationship deepens when Lucy – forced to earn money for payment of the cottage – pens the captain's memoirs, "Blood and Swash". However, when she meets the suave author Miles Fairley (George Sanders) while at the publishing house, the Captain realizes that his "Lucia" may be wanting the love, companionship, and reality of a mortal man.

"Real happiness is worth almost any risk.... but be careful me dear, there may be breakers ahead"

Joseph Mankiewicz's wonderfully whimsical fantasy was released in theatres in 1947 to great commercial success. It was based on the novel, "The Ghost and Mrs. Muir" written two years earlier by author Josephine Leslie, who - like her character Lucy Muir - published her book under a much more masculine pseudonym...R.A. Dick.

20th Century Fox purchased the rights to the story shortly after its publication and selected Philip Dunne to rework it into a fitting screenplay for a feature film. Philip Dunne was a very talented screenwriter who had been nominated for an Academy Award in 1941 for *How Green Was My Valley*. He retained much of the essence of the book, and much of the plot, too - with the exception of eliminating the character of Mrs. Muir's son.

What resulted from his penwork was a sweeping romance like none other of the era. The script, the actors, Mankiewicz's direction, the breathtaking cinematography (by Charles Lang Jr.) and Bernard Herrman's beautifully haunting score all combined to make The Ghost and Mrs. Muir one of the most enchanting, timeless, and delightful films ever made in Hollywood.

Rex Harrison is superb as our beloved sea captain – handsome, brawny, and blazed-eyed....a man in every sense of the word. While Gene Tierney is his perfect mate - beautiful, prim and respectable. What they both shared was the spirit of adventure in their souls.

FAMOUS AND FORGOTTEN FILMS

"How you'd of loved the North Cape and the fjords and the midnight sun...to sail across the reef at Barbados where the blue waters turn to green....to the Falklands, where a southerly gale rips the whole sea white.....Oh, what we've missed Lucia! What we've both missed."

The rest of this excellent cast includes George Sanders (playing his usual deliciously sly self), character actress Edna Best as Mrs. Muir's right hand arm and dear companion Martha, little Natalie Wood as daughter Anna, English stage legend Isobel Elsom as Lucy's mother-in-law, Robert Coote as the real-estate agent, Anna Lee as "the wife", and Austrian actress Vanessa Brown as the grown-up Anna.

While "flesh and blood", Captain Gregg must have been a magnificent seaman and one can imagine the loyalty he inspired in his men aboard ship. Square shouldered, steadfast and weathered

from his voyages, he was wise beyond his years, or as he described himself...

"I did not lead a very wise life but it was a full one and a grown-up one. You come to age very quickly through shipwreck and disaster and at the heart of the whirlpool some men find God."

Lucy Muir is quite an independent woman for the turn-of-the-century. Young, innocent and idealistic, she had married a man who had swept her off her feet, only to discover that he was not the romantic she had thought him to be. After his death, she wants to live a life of her own, free to make decisions without anyone warning her of society's views on her actions. She finds her true self and her peace at Gull Cottage. And there amongst the splendor of the ocean she does not dream of her husband returning to life, but rather of a Gothic hero, a spirit like the Flying Dutchman, a man who worships her as much as the fairest lady he ever knew...the mighty Sea herself.

But is Captain Gregg a dream, or is he a man full of life and vigor just as much as Lucy?

Years later, when Mrs. Muir's hair is white and the driftwood by the beach battered and worn by the crashing tide, she still reflects upon her "dream" of the captain. In spite of being a very beautiful woman, she had chosen to live her days in the seclusion of Gull Cottage. We have the notion that men were not something Mrs. Muir ever pursued again. The ideal nature of the captain and the comradery they shared would be hard for any mere mortal man to duplicate.

Instead, all of Lucy's real relationships are with other women.... her maid being the only lasting friendship she has known. Her daughter has her own life to lead and as she grows older she becomes as remote as the rest of the world that Lucy has turned her back against. But loneliness is something our heroine never knows, for she feels content and secure in her memories and secretly lives in hope of something as real as what she was dreaming of all those years.

In the hands of another director, *The Ghost and Mrs. Muir* may have been a tragic story, a story of lost love and regret and of a woman living out an empty life of isolation. Instead, under the direction of Joseph Mankiewicz, it becomes a magnificent mystical romance. Gentle and warm and humorous, too. It is a tale of love transcending all boundaries.

The Leprechauns say:
"Lovers who kiss under a falling star are bound together forevermore..."

A ROMANCE FRESH... JOYFUL...LILTING AS AN IRISH AIR...TO PUT ENCHANTMENT IN THE VERY HEART OF YOU!

TYRONE **POWER** ANNE **BAXTER**

THE LUCK OF THE IRISH

with
The Little Man **CECIL KELLAWAY**
The Big Man **LEE J. COBB**

20th CENTURY-FOX

JAMES TODD · JAYNE MEADOWS · J. M. KERRIGAN · PHIL BROWN · CHARLES IRWIN
Directed by HENRY KOSTER · Produced by FRED KOHLMAR · Screen Play by Philip Dunne · Based on a Novel by Guy and Constance Jones

20th CENTURY FOX (1948)

THE LUCK OF THE IRISH

"You don't always wait for an invitation to follow the brave music of a distant drum"

It's not often when a man is clever enough and quick enough to capture a leprechaun. While travelling in Ireland, Steven Fitzgerald (Tyrone Power) does just that and then, having done so, lets the leprechaun free...without claiming his pot of gold!

'Tis a rare man indeed who would do such a thing, and the leprechaun knows it. He feels a debt of gratitude to this American and, leaving the comfort of his homeland and his secluded waterfall, he follows him into the "cold, inhospitable city" of New York to serve him and to help him realize his heart's desire.

"You are a proud, free man, and it is for that reason that I am proud to serve you"

Fitzgerald is a news reporter who believes in writing the truth to the public, but the lure of acquiring wealth by working for power-hungry publisher-turned-politician Augur (Lee J. Cobb) proves to be irresistible, even if it costs him his integrity as a free-thinking man. Egging him on in his decision to accept this position is Augur's daughter (Jayne Meadows), a woman who wants to be by Fitzgerald's side as he climbs the ladder of success, no matter what it takes.

The Luck of the Irish is a dramatic fantasy filled with many whimsical moments. It does not have the sugary sweetness of a children's fable, making it all the more satisfying. Instead it has a lasting charm which makes it ideal for annual viewing on St. Patrick's Day, or any time of the year for that matter.

The first half of the film parallels Michael Powell's *I Know Where I'm Going* (1945) in that we see a city dweller stranded in a small village, anxious to escape on the next boat available and frustrated with the local people's slow and inefficient ways. It is not until the opportunity to escape becomes available that these characters begin to have doubts on whether they truly want to leave. In both films, it is the romance they find in these villages which make the

FAMOUS AND FORGOTTEN FILMS

characters wish to remain, not the lure of the tranquil community.

In *The Luck of the Irish*, Fitzgerald meets and falls in love with Nora (Anne Baxter), a quiet innkeeper's daughter, and upon his return to New York he sees her once again, by chance, on a subway. He has a notion that the leprechaun may have had a hand in bringing her to New York but he struggles to relinquish his dream of wealth in place of returning to Ireland with Nora.

"You brought Nora here, didn't you?"

"No, you brought her yourself... in your mind, long ago."

Steven Fitzgerald is an ageless character - working men are forever torn between following the dreams of their heart or selling out their ideals (and sometimes their morals) to other men for the sake of financial stability. He is a cynical man and does not easily get himself beguiled into believing in leprechauns or other folklore but, in this situation, his belief becomes his blessing.

The Luck of the Irish is not your traditional fairy-tale story and the irascible leprechaun with his proverbial pot of gold is not portrayed as a cultural

image but instead becomes the incarnation of Fitzgerald's conscious and a vehicle of divine influence in changing his circumstances. The moral of film is summed up in its tagline "Choosing good is the real pot of gold".

"I offered you gold. 'Tis not my fault that you prefer a pebble"

The Luck of the Irish premiered on September 14, 1948, and for its original showing featured a wee bit o' something green - all of the Ireland sequences were tinted the color of the Irish landscape itself. Indeed, the opening sequences of Ireland are so pleasant that it is a shame when, midway through the film, its focus shifts to New York City.

A roster of 20th Century Fox's regular talents gathered together to make this a stand-out picture: director Henry Koster, who was an old hand at filming humorous dramas; Lyle Wheeler, Fox's resident art director extraordinaire; Philip Dunne, who hammered out on his magical typewriter this whale of a grand adaptation (from the novel by Guy and Constance Jones); and producer Fred Kohler, who had footed the bill one year prior for that other excellent romantic-fantasy The Ghost and Mrs. Muir. The strains of traditional Irish and English melodies can be heard in the background thanks to the musical wizardry of Cyril Mockridge.

Cecil Kellaway steals the film with his performance of "Horace", the leprechaun turned manservant, and he nails the Irish accent and mannerisms of one of the little people. He was nominated for an Academy Award for Best Supporting Actor for his portrayal. James Todd also co-starred as Fitzgerald's wise-cracking pal Bill Clark, and J.M. Kerrigan and Phil Brown round out the stellar cast.

Anne Baxter is particularly fetching and these years were certainly the peak of her career. The brightness of Tyrone Power's star had been waning a few years prior to The Luck of the Irish and he must have sensed that his days of being the studio's No. 1 glamour boy were nearly over, even though he was as handsome as ever. Jayne Meadows related a story about this in the special "Jayne Meadows Remembers" included on the DVD:

> "[in-between takes during the banquet scene] he said, 'You see that tall man over there, the one with the grey hair? He was a star once. A very big star. Sad...now he is an extra'. And I said 'Isn't it wonderful that he's still working' because, you know, the man looked like he needed something to hold him up. When I later found out that Ty started as an extra, I thought 'isn't it interesting that his first reaction was to the old man who was a star and is now an extra.' "

Perhaps Tyrone Power felt that eventually this would be his fate as well.

METRO-GOLDWYN-MAYER (1948)

"The Secret Garden"

"Aye, I know wha' tis said. He locked the gate and buried the key, and nary's been in there since."

A secret garden. It has been locked up for years and is now overgrowing with weeds and bramble for want of anyone to tend to it. When the young orphan Mary Lennox first discovers this enchanted place at the estate of her uncle, she views the garden as an amusing diversion from her loneliness and boredom, but she soon finds that the key that unlocked its door may hold the answer to unlocking the buried secret in her uncle's past.

The Secret Garden was based upon a 1910 novel by the beloved children's book author Frances Hodgson Burnett. To this day it remains her most popular book, along with "Little Lord Fauntleroy" and "The Little Princess", all of which were adapted to film numerous times over the years. The enduring popularity of these stories can be attributed to Burnett's flair for writing about story elements that children find appealing such as mysterious passageways, orphans from exotic lands, strange characters, locked doors, and hidden gardens. Her stories also consistently featured children as the heroes.

Mary Lennox (portrayed by Margaret O'Brien) is a strange heroine, however, for a book or a film. She is bratty and spoiled having been accustomed to servants waiting on her hand and foot in India. After her parents die from cholera, she is shipped off to England to reside in an oppressive mansion with her uncle, Lord Archibald Craven (Herbert Marshall), a bitter brooding man.

Each night, Mary hears a screaming voice echoing through the myriad hallways. The servants attempt to quench her curiosity, explaining it simply as "the wind howling from the moors", but Mary finds that they are coming from the bedchamber of a small boy, Colin Craven (Dean Stockwell), her uncle's son. From constant coddling, Master Craven has become an invalid and, believing that he will grow into a hunchback one day, finds living futile. Mary finds her match in Colin because he, too, is spoiled and prone to screaming tantrums. It is only after Mary befriends Dickon, a

FAMOUS AND FORGOTTEN FILMS

neighbor boy, and discovers the secret garden, that she learns to find contentment in the simple pleasures of life.

The Secret Garden is a Clarence Brown production and his visual style is evident throughout the film, but most of the credit for the quality of the film should be given to director Fred Wilcox who established a wonderful moody atmosphere through great use of light and shadow. As an added touch, a Technicolor sequence was utilized to give that extra emotional punch, while the beautiful Cedric Gibbons sets bring the story to life in a fashion that even location filming could not have equaled.

Metro-Goldwyn-Mayer excelled at adapting novels to lush film productions and, like most of their output in the late 1940s, The Secret Garden featured some of the best talent to be found in Hollywood, both in front and behind the camera. Those tried-and-true child actors, Dean Stockwell and Margaret O'Brien, were excellent in their roles, as was newcomer Brian Roper in the part of Dickon (interestingly, he was 20 years old at the time).

The adult roles are so well cast that one tends to forget that they are mostly caricatures: Dame Gladys Cooper as the stern housekeeper; Elsa Lanchester as the irrepressibly happy maid; dour Reginald Owen as the old nosy gardener. Even the small cameo performances sparkle with Metro's character talents: Billy Bevan as an overheated British soldier in India; Dennis Hoey as Marshall's stern valet; Aubrey Mather and George Zucco as young Stockwell's doctors; and Norma Varden as his wise nurse.

NUGGET REVIEWS

"There's gold in them thar films!"

NANCY DREW AND THE HIDDEN STAIRCASE (1939) *14k*

Someone is trying to scare two old spinsters from their home in order that they may forfeit on their inheritance. Nancy Drew and Ted Nickerson try to help and discover a hidden tunnel in the process. *Bonita Granville, John Litel, Frankie Thomas, Warner Brothers. Directed by William Clemens.*

Some may think the Nancy Drew series of the 1930s were just average run-of-the-mill entertainment, but I've got a soft spot for Nancy and her sleuthing shenanigans and this film ranks as one of my favorites in the series.. How Ted puts up with Nancy is a wonder! She has him chase pidgeons around town, pushes him in a basement to spend a night with a killer, and steals his belt ("You don't seem to understand Nancy...that's the only thing that's keeping my pants up!"). It's a great little mystery and great fun to watch.

STANLEY AND LIVINGSTONE (1939) *14k*

THE MORE THE MERRIER (1943) *18k*

To help relieve the housing shortage in Washington D.C, a young woman rents her single apartment to an old bachelor who in turn sublets his half to a young bachelor with the intention of match-making the two chickadees. *Jean Arthur, Joel McCrea, Charles Coburn, Richard Gaines. Columbia Pictures. Directed by George Stevens.*

The More the Merrier is one of George Stevens' most famous comedies, and justly so, for it is a gem of a great film and you'll have a hard time containing your laughter during the first half-hour. After that, however, things start getting a little zany and the humor becomes less-visual and more verbal, which - in the opinion of this fan - isn't quite as entertaining as pie-in-the-face comedy. Jean Arthur gets top-billing, but it is jiggle-jowled Charles Coburn who steals all the scenes in his role of Mr. Dingle. Cary Grant came no where near imitating Coburn's natural comedic talent when he took on the role of the aged cupid in the 1966 remake, *Walk Don't Run.*

New York Herald reporter Henry Stanley is assigned to deepest darkest Africa to discover whether Dr. Livingstone is still living or not. The Herald's competing newspaper, The London Globe, claims he is dead. *Spencer Tracy, Charles Coburn, Walter Brennan, Cedric Hardwicke, Nancy Kelly, and Richard Greene.*

Spencer Tracy really enjoyed picking meaty roles in the 1930s. This one he got to sink his teeth firmly into and did quite well with it....until his character came to the realization of the importance of spiritual matters. Here, Tracy floundered and couldn't quite convince the audience of his transformation. Acting can only go so far, Mr. Tracy. Walter Brennan and Charles Coburn are splendid supports, and overall this is a really fine adventure film. Makes one feel like trekking across Africa even today!

THE ARCHERS (1949)

THE SMALL BACK ROOM

In the midst of World War II, bomb expert and research scientist Sammy Rice (David Farrar) is recruited by Army captain Dick Stuart (Michael Gough) to investigate a dangerous new bomb that the Germans are scattering throughout Britain's beaches. Sammy struggles with alcoholism and a sense of worthlessness because of a recent injury which left him with a wooden leg, but when he puts his life on the line to disengage one of these bombs he realizes just how beautiful life is - even with a game leg.

Director Michael Powell and screenwriter Emeric Pressburger made a number of excellent dramas in the 1940s which they released under the banner of their production company The Archers. The most famous of these films (*A Matter of Life and Death, Black Narcissus, The Red Shoes*) were beautifully shot in Technicolor by cinematographer Jack Cardiff.

After the color explosion that audiences witnessed in *The Red Shoes*, Powell decided to

return to using black and white film, which the Archers were known for throughout the 1930s. This was a good choice for it emphasized the despair and the struggles that our hero, Sammy, was facing. Adding to his worries, the research department that he works for happens to be undergoing a shift in management and Sammy feels that his prospects for the future seem as bleak as the work environment he is accustomed to. The title *The Small Back Room* cleverly refers to the department's makeshift offices. In the U.S, the film was released as *Hour of Glory*, an equally fitting title.

FAMOUS AND FORGOTTEN FILMS

Like most of the Powell/Pressburger films, *The Small Back Room* features stunning camerawork (Christopher Challis was the cinematographer) and moving performances from all of the principal players, especially from underrated actor David Farrar. However, the film lacks the momentum of the Archer's other pictures. The mystery of the German bombs that are being randomly dropped throughout Britain is the thread that binds the story and yet it seems to be hidden among the tangled netting of Sammy's personal travails until the final quarter of the picture. His struggle with self-worth and his romance with Susan, a secretary, take center stage instead.

Kathleen Byron, another underrated actress (and one of Michael Powell's favorite players) portrays this secretary. This character is quite unlike the neurotic Sister Ruth that Byron is famous for playing in *Black Narcissus* (1947). Susan is a lovely woman who stands behind Sammy in his moments of darkness.

The Small Back Room is not one of Powell and Pressburger's best works but it has its moments of glory and it offers an insightful look into the emotional/moral struggles that many of the "back room boys" must have been wrestling with during the war. Cyril Cusack, Jack Hawkins, and Leslie Banks also star.

UNIVERSAL PICTURES (1950)

BROKEN ARROW

Broken Arrow was the first dramatic western that James Stewart ever made and he was so well suited to the genre that he went on to star in sixteen more westerns within the next 25 years. The story is one of friendship, love, and cultural understanding set against the backdrop of the tumultuous Apache Wars in the Arizona Territory in 1870.

James Stewart portrays veteran scout Tom Jeffords who is tired of the warfare between the whites and the Apaches. He reasons that intelligence and understanding must be used in putting a halt to the war. He learns the Apache language and their customs and then rides into their camp to prevail upon their leader Cochise to allow the overland mail riders to pass unharmed. This is a small step in what Tom hopes will be the beginning of peace negotiations.

Jeffords slowly gains the trust of Cochise who agrees to talk peace terms with General Oliver Otis Howard who is acting as an ambassador to the "Great White Chief", President Ulysses S. Grant. Cochise eventually agrees to "break the arrow" with the white people, a symbol of the Apaches to stop fighting, but there are men on both sides who resist extending the olive branch of peace.

"To talk of peace is not hard. To live it is very hard."

If you enjoy action-packed westerns, then *Broken Arrow* is not for you. It meanders along like a gentle brook and the only tension to be had is in wondering whether the peace treaty will be broken by either party before they have a chance to cement their relationship. However, the story is so engrossing that action is not needed. It is a touching and thought-provoking film. When Tom first enters Apache territory, he expects to encounter a hostile warrior and isn't even certain he will leave the area alive. Instead, he finds a man as tired of war as he is. Cochise admires Jeffords courage in approaching his camp and is touched that he took the time and effort to learn the Apache language and way of life. In turn, Jeffords comes to respect Cochise and the care he has for his people. A strong bond is forged between him and Cochise, one built on mutual admiration.

Jeff Chandler gives a wonderful and dignified performance as the wise warrior. He was such a handsome man and had a natural flair for acting. With his expressive face, minimal dialogue was needed for him to convey a message, making him an ideal actor for this role. Cochise was a man who used actions instead of words. Chandler was nominated for an Academy Award for his role and - according to Kim Newman, author of "Wild West Movies" - he established Cochise as the "1950s model of an Indian hero."

James Stewart also gives a sensitive performance as the weary scout. Jeffords is a middle-aged man who has been alone all of his life. Now that he is getting older, all he wants is peace and the settler's life he never had. When he enters Apache Territory the last thing he expects to find is romance, but he falls in love with the beautiful Sonseeahray (16-year-old Debra Paget making her screen debut) the moment he sees her and asks Cochise for her hand in marriage.

"It won't be easy for you both....You will go far away, always to new places but your eyes will never see anything because they will always be turned backwards... towards home."

Also in the cast is Basil Ruysdael as the "Christian General", Jay Silverheels as Geronimo, and Frank McGrath. Delmar Daves does a wonderful job directing the film and creating a compelling narrative. This was the first western he directed and it inspired a genre of "pro-Indian" films in the 1950s. The cinematography is also beautiful and captures the breathtaking beauty of the American Southwest with its desert landscapes and majestic mountains.

FAMOUS AND FORGOTTEN FILMS

"Nothing can change our love... neither the color of your skin— nor mine!"

For the first time, the screen portrays the poignant love story of a white man and an Indian girl that broke all barriers of color and hate.

Broken Arrow was based on the 1947 novel "Blood Brother" by Elliott Arnold which, in turn, was based on a true occurrence between Cochise and frontier scout Tom Jeffords, who was also the superintendent of the overland mail in Arizona Territory in the 1860s. The film was notable at the time for being one of the first Westerns to show a compassionate view of the Native Americans.

Shortly after filming wrapped, James Stewart began work on *Winchester '73* directed by Anthony Mann. This would be the first of six westerns he would make with Mann in the 1950s. *Broken Arrow* and *Winchester '73* were released within two months of each other in the summer of 1950 and both were box-office hits. *Broken Arrow* was nominated for three Academy Awards and also earned a Golden Globe for Best Film Promoting International Understanding.

WARNER BROTHERS (1950)

ALFRED HITCHCOCK'S "STAGE FRIGHT"

"Hands that applaud can also kill!"

The stage is set. The curtain is drawn. Act One begins. Eve Gill (Jane Wyman) is helping fellow dramatic art student Jonathan Cooper (Richard Todd) escape to her father's coastal home to hide out until they can smuggle him across to Scotland. He is in an awful jam you see, as he explains to Eve he has just unwillingly become the prime suspect in the murder of flamboyant stage actress Charlotte Inwood's husband. In a flashback of his account we see how Charlotte manipulated him, her lover, into returning to her townhouse to fetch a dress after she had stained her own with blood while bludgeoning her husband with a fire-poker, only to be seen by Inwood's maid before fleeing.

Eve sets out to prove his innocence and with the help of her father and Detective Smith (Michael Wilding) lead the police to whom she believes to be the real murderer - Charlotte Inwood (Marlene Dietrich).

Stage Fright was released on February 23rd, 1950 and marked the first picture in a four film contract agreement Hitchcock had signed with Warner Brothers. While it garnered rave reviews by critics it was rather harshly received by the general public due to the key element in this intriguing film - the false flashback. Hitchcock himself dismissed the film in later years because of this flashback, a technique he considered was the second worst directorial mistake he had ever made in his career.

Alfred Hitchcock had gained notoriety as a suspense film director in the UK as far back as the mid 1930s with such films as *The Lodger* and *The Lady Vanishes*. It was not until the early 1940s that he became known in America making such hits as *Suspicion*, *Notorious*, *Lifeboat* and *Shadow of a Doubt*.

Stage Fright was a sojourn back to his native land. It was filmed entirely in England at Associated British Pathe Studios and boasts a superb English cast. Michael Wilding, a very charismatic actor who was popular overseas in his frequent pairings with Anna Neagle, plays a dapper gentleman detective named Smith who has his eye - and heart - on Eve. Alastair Sim, one of England's most engaging character actors, costars as Commodore Rill, Eve's father, who fancies himself a notorious criminal for having once smuggled two cases of brandy across the Scottish border. Dame Sybil Thorndike portrays Mrs. Gill, Eve's mother, a very dotty mother whose prim and properness contrast starkly with those of her husband, the Commodore.

"Forgiveness is the secret of a happy marriage...that and good long stretches of the absence that makes a heart grow fonder." - *Commodore Rill*

Although *Stage Fright* is mild in suspense it more than makes up for it in sheer entertainment. For viewers, it is a leisurely stroll to capture a criminal versus an energetic race to clear the guilt of an innocent man and we are sidetracked along the way by some delightful little characterizations by Kay Walsh and Miles Malleson, as well as Joyce Grenfell doing a wonderful guest appearance as a shooting booth attendant at a theatrical garden party.

Richard Todd had previously scored a hit in the WWII drama *The Hasty Heart* (1949) and was fast becoming a leading star. Why Hitchcock chose not to use him in other films remains a mystery. His portrayal of the distraught Jonathan Cooper is quite chilling. Today, *The Dam Busters* (1955) remains his most recognized movie although he made many other excellent films throughout the 1950s including several Walt Disney live-action films.

"She made me do it! Don't you see? I had no other choice"

Jane Wyman was dressed down for her role as Eve and plays a soft-spoken young lady who endangers herself for the sake of the man she believes she loves. When "ordinary Smith" comes into her life her affections take a new direction though. Marlene Dietrich, on the other hand, is as Dietrichesque as ever as Charlotte Inwood and is especially alluring in her final scene. Cole Porter wrote the song "The Laziest Gal in Town" for her one musical number in the film and it remained a signature song in her repertoire until her final days.

Strangers on a Train would be Hitchcock's next picture and its success, both critically and commercially, would knock *Stage Fright* away from the spotlight to the back rows of obscurity. Nevertheless, it is an underrated gem from the Master of Suspense and deserves to be recognized among his fans for its charm and character, if not for its "fright."

Check it out!
If you like this, you'll also like.....

Dial M for Murder (1954)

Elaborate Alfred Hitchcock thriller with Ray Milland as Tony Wendice, a tennis pro who plots to commit the "perfect" crime: the murder of his unfaithful wife, Margot (Grace Kelly). But Margot defends herself against the man sent to do her in, killing him instead. Now, with his plan slowly beginning to unravel, Tony is forced to do some quick thinking. With Robert Cummings, John Williams.

LUX FILM (1951)

ANNA

Silvana Mangano was a beautiful and talented actress who was popular in Italian films of the 1950s, when Italy was going through its post-war film renaissance. This sensuous bombshell ascended to stardom after a sizzling performance in the 1949 drama *Bitter Rice*. She married Dino De Laurentiis, an emerging producer, and he cast her in some fine films, one of which was *Anna* (1951).

This melodrama, like many Italian films, conveys raw emotions in such a frank and simple manner. The story switches back and forth between the present life of novice nun Sister Anna (Mangano), who works as a nurse at a busy hospital in Milano, and her steamy past life. Anna was a nightclub entertainer at a popular cafe. She had a sexual yen for Vittorio (Vittorio Gassman) and would often spend her nights with him. One day, she meets a rich farmer named Andrea (Raf Vallone) who does not see her as an easy pick-up but respects her and treats her as the beautiful young woman she is.

After a brief courtship, he asks her to visit his mother and proposes marriage, but Anna, who is still spending her nights with Vittorio, feels unworthy of the gentle-hearted Andrea. It is this unworthiness that eventually leads her to become a nun - or so we are led to think. What makes *Anna* such an interesting film is that there is a lot of unspoken dialogue which makes it ripe for interpreting the story in various ways.

Anna may have chosen to become a nun because she felt she was a "bad influence" and would never have made Andrea a good wife, or it may have been because she felt a true calling to help others as a nurse. She hints several times that this is the reason and yet she makes her decision to join the holy order prior to knowing anything about nursing. It seems as though it is the confinement of the walls of the hospital that appeals to her more, or perhaps the chance to atone for her past through service to others.

Anna was beautifully filmed by director Alberto Lattuada. It is a wonderfully soapy melodrama bubbling over with fine performances from all of the principal cast members. Silvana Mangano gives an especially appealing performance. She was such a beauty in her time and, like many of the stars of silent era pictures, she was able to convey so much through her eyes alone.

"*Bitter Rice*"
introducing the new star
SILVANA MANGANO

Raf Vallone, the leading man, was a handsome actor with great virility. Unlike actors such as Marcello Mastroianni or Vittorio Gassmann, Raf Vallone does not look like a movie star. He was a representative of Italy's "everyman" and often took on roles of commoners: farmers, soldiers, miners, and machinists. No matter what role he was given or how brief it was, he always made a memorable impression.

Vittorio Gassmann, Raf Vallone, and Silvana Mangano all had major roles in *Bitter Rice*, so *Anna* marked a reunion for these actors. Also starring in the film are Silvana Mangano's two sisters: Patrizia, who plays Anna's sister Luisa, and Natascia, who portrays Andrea's younger sister. The wonderful actress and voice-over performer Tina Lattanzi is Andrea's mother and two great

French actors, Jacques Dumesnil and Gaby Morlay, play in the hospital sequences as, respectably, the doctor and Mother Superior.

Anna also features two excellent nightclub music sequences where Silvana dances and sings to the beautiful "Non Dimenticar," which was popularized in the US by Nat King Cole, and the enticing baião "El Negro Zumbon.". This song became an instant classic in Italy and Spain, but it was not until 2004 that American audiences heard it through Pink Martini's rendition.

Anna is often overshadowed by other Italian film classics of the era, but it was a huge commercial success at the time and its entertainment value has not diminished over the years.

PARAMOUNT PICTURES (1951)

Darling, How Could You!

Scottish novelist James M. Barrie is today best remembered for penning the classic children's story "Peter Pan" (1905), but during the turn-of-the-century he was one of the most popular playwrights in England, writing such plays as "The Little Minister," "Quality Street," and "The Admirable Crichton." He had a flair for comedy and one of his best comedic plays "Alice-Sit-by-the-Fire" (1905) - a story of a couple's reunion with their children after several years absence - was brought to the screen in 1951 as the charming *Darling, How Could You!* starring John Lund and Joan Fontaine.

Dr. Mark Gray (Lund) and his wife Alice (Fontaine) return home to Boston after having spent five years in Panama aiding in the yellow fever epidemic during the construction of the Panama Canal in 1900. Their three children, Amy (Mona Freeman), Cosmo (David Stollery), and baby Molly (Maureen Lynn Reimer), had remained in Boston and were being cared for by Mark's mother and a nursemaid (Angela Clarke).

Both Mark and Alice are impatient to be reunited with their children, but while Mark builds a rapport with the children in a snap, Alice is overly-anxious for instant love and finds the initial greetings awkward. She also has to contend with jealousy from the nursemaid who grew attached to baby Molly while they were away. Meanwhile, their imaginative daughter Amy is convinced their mother is having an affair with a friend of the family (Peter Hansen) after having accidentally seen a theatrical play that portrayed the "seamy side of life".

Darling, How Could You! is a little-remembered comedy today and yet it boasts a great cast of pros that handle their parts with ease and features some very humorous moments... two qualities which should make it more memorable. While the film starts off rather slow it builds up considerably when Lund and Fontaine enter the scene and ends with a tickling good comedic sequence involving Alice's misunderstood romantic entanglement.

John Lund is especially charming as the understanding Victorian father of the family. He cuts a dashing figure and is an admirably loving husband to Alice. Joan Fontaine didn't often get a chance to play comedy parts so she tackled her role with gusto and looked particularly beautiful while doing so. And the children were perfectly cast: David Stollery, later a veteran of Walt Disney television series such as *Spin and Marty*, is adorable as Cosmo, their little tough-talking son, while the underrated Mona Freeman displays perfect comedic timing as their winsome teenage daughter Amy.

It may seem strange today that any young couple would choose to be separated from their children, but James Barrie's original play was set in London with the Grays returning home from British India. It was quite common at the time for couples who were residing in India to send their children back to England to be cared for by family members or nannies due to the risk of disease or uprisings in India. For the film, the setting was changed to Boston to appeal to American audiences, and so the yellow fever epidemic in Panama was given as the reason for the Grays absence for such a long period. Pretty clever.

20th CENTURY FOX (1951)

Mr. Belvedere Rings the Bell

In 1948, 20th Century Fox released *Sitting Pretty*, a comedy featuring a character named Lynn Belvedere who was unlike any other that ever appeared in books, radio, or film. Belvedere was an author and lecturer and a very well-educated snob. He didn't just know a little bit about everything, he was an authority in every field. Mr. Belvedere was a bonafide genius and knew it. He was terribly vain and would make sure that everyone else knew he was a genius as well.

"I have a very ordinary face. It's only my eyes that reveal my amazing intelligence."

Belvedere had a keen wit, a superior air, and a biting tongue that could quickly put others in their proper place: beneath him.

The one quality that Mr. Belvedere had and did not often boast about was his benevolence. Under his crusty exterior, he was a do-gooder at heart and delighted in helping those whom he deemed worthy of his aid.

In *Sitting Pretty*, Clifton Webb portrayed Mr. Belvedere, and he was able to convey both of these sides of his nature brilliantly. Very few actors could have tackled this part, yet Webb did so easily and made Belvedere an all-around lovable character.

FAMOUS AND FORGOTTEN FILMS

Sitting Pretty had Mr. Belvedere take on the job of a nanny and attempt to prove that he could raise three rambunctious children better than their parents. The film was such a hit at the box office, that Fox followed it up with two more Mr. Belvedere pictures.

Mr. Belvedere Rings the Bell, released in 1951, was the third in the series and the best of the three. It was also unique for featuring a plot set in the unlikeliest of places - a nursing home.

While on a lecture tour, Belvedere overhears some elderly people in a park complaining about life and their various ailments. The idea of getting old before his time intrigues him and he wonders whether there is "any point in living to be 80."

Being the man of action that he is, he abandons his tour - much to the chagrin of his publicity agent (Zero Mostel) - and decides to enter himself into the Church of John Home for the Aged to see what life in a nursing home is like. Entrance is not as easy as it seems for they do not accept people under 70. But fortune favors the bold and Mr. Belvedere is mistaken to be a Mr. Erwenter, a 77-

year-old man who had already enrolled... so he simply assumes his identity.

The inhabitants of the old age home welcome him with excitement because "Mr. Erwenter" isn't a bit like themselves. He has a zest for living and, strangely enough, doesn't look like he is 77 years old at all!

"We're very happy to have you with us, Mr. Erwenter. It will make a nice change." - *Nurse Harriet*

"You've no idea how much of a change it will make!" - *Mr. Belvedere*

Belvedere's original intention in coming to the Church of John may have been to preview his future but once he arrives and sees the downhearted spirits of his fellow lodgers, he makes up his mind to become an instigator of change, an intentional gust of wind to stir their minds and blow new life into their dull and uneventful lives.

FAMOUS AND FORGOTTEN FILMS

Each of the inhabitants is touched in a profound way by this one man. Mr. Beebe (Billy Lynn) is especially affected by Belvedere's arrival. Mr. Beebe has no interest in life. He is waiting for spring, even while knowing that the spring to come will only resemble the winter that was.

Mr. Cherry (Harry Hines) is downhearted, too. He eats the food that is set before him but wishes the church had the funds to buy him a new set of teeth. Ms. Hoadley drinks ("Nobody has a right to be that happy," a fellow lodger comments); Ms. Sampler only talks of "love, love, love" and the three marriages she had; and saddest of all is Mrs. Hammer (Doro Merande) who hides her loneliness behind snarky - although amusing - remarks.

"Eat and sleep, sleep and eat. The only action we get around here is in our stomachs."

Nurse Harriet (Joanne Dru) always has a cheerful smile and tries her best to tend to their needs and liven their spirits. "Someday we'll have a wonderful garden with green grass and pretty flowers," she says. "Flowers won't grow here. The whole place is old, even the ground. You ought to be ashamed to run an old dump," Mrs. Hammer replies.

Harriet is in love with Reverend Watson (Hugh Marlowe) but he seems oblivious to her. The reverend wants the best for the elderly left in his charge but he has become so preoccupied with bills and the needs of the church that he has neglected their spiritual needs.

"Bills, bills, bills! Religion has become so expensive, only the wicked can afford it."

They all need a shot of vitality and this is what Mr. Erwenter aka Mr. Belvedere provides in the form of a secret youth potion. He tells them of the days he spent with the great Lo Chin Po, a 112-year-old Tibetan, and how together they discovered a formula for restoring youth. "I will write to Lo Chin Po and ask him to send me some more pills for you," Mr. Erwenter announces. The excitement of the thought of being young again makes everyone come alive.

Mr. Erwenter also arranges a bazaar to help the church raise money for Mr. Cherry's new set of teeth and Mrs. Hammer's appendix operation. He gives them all something to look forward to, a new lease on life. But the happiness they feel and their faith in Mr. Erwenter crumble suddenly when they discover that he is not Mr. Erwenter at all, but a 45-year-old author named Mr. Belvedere who has been "feeding us lies."

With a plot such as this you would imagine that *Mr. Belvedere Rings the Bell* is a depressing film to watch. After all, it is set in a rundown nursing home filled with characters who are waiting to die. But it is quite the contrary - it is a gem of a comedy. The script, by Ranald MacDougall, is marvelously witty and benefits from having talented character actors deliver the lines with such humor.

Doro Merande is especially wonderful in the role of bitter Mrs. Hammer. Most of the actors were much younger than the characters they were playing but they tottered around looking convincingly old. Billy Lynn, as Mr. Beebe, gives a touching performance of a heartbroken old man. Like a child who just discovered that Santa Claus is only a fable, Mr. Beebe is hurt more so than the others by Mr. Belvedere's "betrayal" because he had the most faith in him.

"Being young is the way you think! Live every moment as if it is going to be the last one you will ever have. Believe you're young and you will be young. That's my secret." - *Mr. Belvedere*

Hugh Marlowe is wonderful as always as the kindly minister whose life and outlook of life is changed by Belvedere's arrival, and Joanne Dru, as Harriet, is a lovely ray of sunshine in their bleak world. Also in the cast are Warren Stevens, Jane Marbury, and Hugh Beaumont as a policeman.

The story was based on the play "The Silver Whistle" by Robert E. McEnroe, which featured a cheerful hobo named Wilfred Tasbinder who takes on the persona of Mr. Erwenter and helps the lives of those in a nursing home. Ranald MacDougall took the character of Belvedere from Gwen Davenport's 1947 novel and blended him into McEnroe's story, sprinkling the script with wry humor.

20th Century Fox released a number of fine light-hearted comedies like this in the late 1940s and early 1950s. They all were given a healthy budget and a great production staff. Henry Koster *(The Luck of the Irish, Harvey)* was put in charge of directing *Mr. Belvedere Rings the Bell* and he had a marvelous flair for making films that were both sentimental and humorous...and shared a message. This picture was ideal for his talents and featured a story about a beneficial intruder not unlike the leading characters found in *The Bishop's Wife* and *Come to the Stable*, both of which he directed.

Mr. Belvedere Rings the Bell has a beautiful message about enjoying life and making every moment count. At one point in the film, Belvedere asks Harriet, "It's close to 10 o'clock now. 9 o'clock is gone and we can never bring it back and live it over. What have you done with the thousands of moments in the past two years?" This question is directed at Harriet the nurse and yet it is asked of the audience as well. Mr. Belvedere, in his vast 45 years of age, has lived a full life. In the one brief week he spends at the Church of John Home of the Aged, he stepped into the lives of the people there unexpectedly and touched each one with his presence. With the thousands of moments we all have, it makes you wonder if you cannot do the same and see how rich life can be.

Mister 880 (1950)

The U.S. Treasury's most implacable adversary is charming, aged counterfeiter "Skipper" Miller (Edmund Gwenn) who knocks out just enough phony singles to live on--and who's eluded capture for a decade. A newly minted Secret Serviceman (Burt Lancaster) takes on the challenge, but can he bring himself to bring the old gent in? Dorothy McGuire co-stars in this charming comedy.

UNITED ARTISTS (1951)

A MAGNIFICENT ADVENTURE IN ENTERTAINMENT!
"THE RIVER"

Jean Renoir is often revered for directing two brilliant cinematographic films of the 1930s - *La Grande Illusion* (1937) and *The Rules of the Game* (1939) - both considered by critics to be among the greatest films ever made, but Renoir also voyaged into the realm of Technicolor in the early 1950s and produced what could be considered one of the most vibrant color films ever made - *The River* (1951), shot entirely in India.

This film won the International prize at the Venice Film Festival when it was first released, but it has since fallen into obscurity, especially among Hollywood film fans. It may be because Renoir chose to use amateur actors for the leads, and while they handle their parts adequately, many feel that their performances kept this film from becoming the classic it could have been.

I feel their naturalness adds to the charm of the picture, which often takes on the tone of a documentary. *The River* is one woman's reminiscences about her childhood in India and the growing pains she encountered as a girl: that woman being Rumer Godden. She was not a glamorous girl, and felt awkward at times... hence, the actress chosen to portray her (Bengal-native Patricia Walters) was not glamorous and often awkward herself.

The other main characters in her story are her childhood friends, Melanie (Radha), an Anglo-Indian girl, and Valerie (Adrienne Corri), a flighty beauty who isn't sure where her emotions stem from. Their peaceful childhood together growing up among the banks of the Bengal river are disrupted when a soldier, Captain John

(Thomas Breen) comes for a prolonged visit with their neighbor. The captain is a handsome youth with flaming red hair, and the three girls quickly become smitten with him. Little do they realize that their romantic fantasies aren't shared by him. Captain John lost a leg in the war, and he has come to India primarily to escape the pity he feared he would receive back home. He also hopes to find inner peace and an acceptance for his condition, but leaves finding neither.

All of the characters in *The River* are truly misfits. Melanie does not know whether her viewpoints about life and marriage are more Eastern or Western; Valerie is beautiful but immature. The main character, Harriet, is wise but homely in appearance; Harriet's father has only one eye; and Captain John is the most lamentable of them all for he feels that his missing leg makes him less whole than others.

Captain John is portrayed by Thomas Breen, son of Joseph I. Breen, a film censor who was appointed by Hays to enforce the Production Code in Hollywood. Thomas had his leg amputated after injuring it in combat in Guam during World War II. Esmond Knight and Nora Swinburne, two prolific English actors, portray Harriet's parents. They lend a touch of professionalism to an otherwise all-amateur cast.

The River is a gentle and thoughtful film and it meanders along at a refreshingly slow pace while it explores these themes of love and hatred, acceptance of our situation, as well as life and death. Renoir makes his audience feel as though they were taking a slow boat journey down the river with plenty of time to stop and observe the locals in their daily activities and meditate on the constancy of the circle of life. If you have the time, it is well worth taking this journey.

METRO-GOLDWYN-MAYER (1952)

"He was born with the gift of laughter and the sense that the world was mad"

Within the last century, Raphael Sabatini's classic 1921 novel "Scaramouche" was made into three film adaptations, including a 1956 television series, but hands down this Metro-Goldwyn-Mayer version starring the engaging English actor Stewart Granger tops them all. The film accomplished that rare feat of improving upon the novel it was based on. *Scaramouche* ranks as one of the best swashbuckling films of the 1950s, and even boasts the longest and most intricate fencing duel in Hollywood's history.

Stewart Granger stars as dashing hero Andre-Louis Moreau, a young lawyer who dedicates years of his life to avenge the death of his best friend (Richard Anderson) who was killed in a duel by the

Marquis de la Tour d'Azyr (Mel Ferrer), a master swordsman. He joins a traveling theatre group where he dons the mask of Scaramouche, the star comedian, in order to hide from the Marquis' soldiers who have ordered Andre arrested as a revolutionary. Even with his dogged determination to pin down the Marquis, Andre takes time off from his fencing lessons to woo Lenore (Eleanor Parker), a flaming red-headed actress and Aline de Gavrillac (Janet Leigh), the pretty young ward of the Marquis.

"But who is Scaramouche? And why does he hide his face behind a mask?"

Scaramouche plunges the audience right into the action from the on-start, packing a lot of story in its 115-minute run time. It features a marvelous cast, excellent cinematography, stunning costumes by Giles Steele, beautiful Cedric Gibbons sets, and a lovely Victor Young score (the end music is especially apropos). In short, it's a rousing good swashbuckler!

Veteran director George Sidney, who was especially adept at filming musicals *(Anchors Aweigh, The Harvey Girls, Annie Get Your Gun, Kiss Me Kate)*, took the helm of this classic, staging all of the sword-fighting sequences as though they were dance numbers. These fencing "ballets" are a highlight of this colorful film and the climatic eight-minute duel sequence between Granger and Ferrer is justly famous for it took these actors eight weeks of training to get their fencing movements precise.

"Scaramouche, you have just given your last performance!"

European fencing champion Jean Heremans provided Stewart Granger with fencing lessons and he delighted in doing all of his own stunts. Granger was ideally cast as the rakish lad born with the gift of laughter. He brought a playful exuberance to the character which was a key element in bringing Sabatini's novel to life.

Granger had seen the original 1923 silent version (starring Ramon Navarro and Lewis Stone) as a child and when he was offered a contract by MGM, he signed it on the condition that Scaramouche would be developed as a project for him.

The studio had toyed with remaking the film for years, first in 1938 with Fernand Gravet, and then as a possible musical version with Gene Kelly or Fernando Lamas in the starring role, so when Granger suggested the book as a vehicle for himself it was swiftly

put into production. Since MGM studios always treated novel-based films with reverence, *Scaramouche* went to the top of their release schedule as an A-picture.

Elizabeth Taylor was originally slated to play the part of Aline de Gavrillac, but had to turn down the role because she was already signed for another picture. Ava Gardner was also to have been in the film, in Eleanor Parker's role. However, this was a fortunate swap for Eleanor Parker is excellent as the feisty Lenore.

Rounding out the cast is Henry Wilcoxon, Nina Foch (as Marie Antoinette), Lewis Stone, Robert Coote, and Elisabeth Risdon.

UNIVERSAL PICTURES (1953)

"ALL I DESIRE"

Naomi Murdoch is returning to the small town of Riverdale to see her daughter perform in a high school play and the town is in a gossiping uproar. Nearly ten years earlier, Naomi left Riverdale, her husband Henry (Richard Carlson), and her three children to pursue a career on the stage as an actress. The townsfolk - and her family - have not forgiven her... all except Lily (Lori Nelson), Naomi's younger daughter. It was a letter from Lily that brought Naomi on her homeward journey.

Once back in Riverdale, Naomi comes to realize how much she has missed her family and her home. But she feels that it is too late to make amends. Henry and she argue the first night she arrives and their eldest daughter Joyce (Marcia Henderson) is particularly bitter towards her. To make matters worse, Dutch Heinemann (Lyle Bettger), a local shop owner, thinks that because Naomi is back in town they can pick up where they left off with their affair.

All I Desire was directed by Douglas Sirk and, like most of his films from the 1950s, it is bubbling with soapy melodrama. Most of his films were shot in color, but this one was black-and-white and it was a good decision to film it in monochrome because of the emphasis it gives to the low lighting and shadows that were

beautifully captured by cinematographer Carl Guthrie (*Caged*).

The script was an adaptation of Carol Brinks' novel "Stopover" and, even though the film's runtime is only 80 minutes, it manages to pack in quite a lot of drama in such a short span - with, surprisingly, no loose ends.

Barbara Stanwyck was ideally cast as Naomi and looks stunning in the turn-of-the-century period costumes designed by Rosemary Odell. Naomi is a weary, hardened woman who never truly achieved success in the theater world yet she chooses to portray herself as an elegant and distinguished actress to make her family proud. Few actresses could have embodied this role with as much conviction as Ms. Stanwyck.

Richard Carlson is also well-suited in the role of Henry, the mild-mannered school principal who is shocked by his wife's return. Henry was beginning to grow attached to Ms. Harper (Maureen

O'Sullivan), the school's drama teacher, but when Naomi comes back into his life, he has to re-evaluate his feelings.

Also in the cast is Billy Gray as Naomi's son Ted, Lotte Stein as the Swedish housekeeper, and Richard Long as Joyce's charming beau. Stuart Whitman and Guy Williams have small parts as Lily's school companions.

The publicity department at 20th Century Fox probably thought that the film's period setting would turn away audience members and so they created poster art that, amusingly, had nothing to do with the film. One poster has a background of storm clouds while a man (presumably Richard Carlson) kisses the neck of a negligee-clad woman who looks a lot like Barbara Hale. Another has a dark-haired Barbara Stanwyck cradling the head of Robert Mitchum, both of them wearing outfits that look like they came out of the 1940s!

All I Desire did not need the pulp-fiction publicity to sell it, because the film is a fine production all around and is one of Barbara Stanwyck's best films of the 1950s.

20th CENTURY FOX (1953)

TITANIC

On April 15th, 1912, in the early morning hours, the luxury liner RMS Titanic sank in the waters of the North Atlantic after striking an iceberg. Over 1,500 passengers perished in one of the worst ocean disasters in history.

Jean Negulesco's Oscar-nominated drama *Titanic* (1953) was not the first film telling of the famous tragedy, but it certainly ranks as one of the best with its lush setting and star-studded cast. Clifton Webb and Barbara Stanwyck star as an unhappily married couple who struggle with family issues onboard the Titanic. These issues suddenly don't seem very serious when they face perishing in the icy waters. Traveling with them is their daughter Annette (Audrey Dalton), a young and beautiful socialite, and their son Norman (Harper Carter), a bright lad who is devoted to his father. Julia (Barbara Stanwyck) thinks her husband Richard is an elegant snob with very little character and sees that their children are becoming just as pompous as he, so she is whisking them off to America to get them away from the European society environment they are used to. Richard boldly sneaks onboard the ship and connives to lure the children back but when the iceberg hits the Titanic, he realizes their safety is more important than anything else.

The story of this family may be fictional but it plays out within a framework of facts. The opening sequence states that "All navigational details of this film - conversations, incidents, and general data - are taken verbatim from the published reports of inquiries held in 1912 by the Congress of the United States and the British Board of Trade."

Titanic was one of 20th Century Fox's top productions of 1953 and it is clearly evident that all involved did their research in making the film historically accurate. The RMS Titanic sets are so meticulously crafted that the ship itself takes the center spotlight in every scene. Stanwyck probably never dreamt that she would have to vie with set props for the audience's attention.

Lyle Wheeler, Maurice Ransford, and Stuart Reiss won an Academy Award nomination for their work on the film's art and set direction and must be applauded for their marvelous special effects, too, which included the sinking of a 22-foot model of the liner.

Charles Brackett and Walter Reisch penned a great tear-inducing script that holds your attention from the start. It is amazing how

FAMOUS AND FORGOTTEN FILMS

much drama is packed into this picture considering its runtime is half the length of James Cameron's 1997 telling of the Titanic.

The film also boasts a stellar cast of supporting players and character actors including a young and handsome Robert Wagner, Richard Basehart, Brian Aherne as the ship's Captain Smith, Thelma Ritter in a "Molly Brown"-ish role, Allyn Joslyn, and Frances Bergen.

METRO-GOLDWYN-MAYER (1954)

BRIGADOON

"If you love someone deeply enough, anything is possible."

'Tis true. Tommy Albright (Gene Kelly) learns just how powerful love is when he comes to the enchanted village of Brigadoon and meets his true love Fiona (Cyd Charisse). Tommy and his friend Jeff Douglas (Van Johnson) come across the village when they are lost in Scotland during a hunting trip. Life in Brigadoon, which only appears for one day every 100 years, is unchanged since the 1700s. Tommy meets and falls in love with the beautiful Fiona and then must make the decision whether to stay in the magical world of Brigadoon and turn his back on the world he knows or whether to depart from it forever.

"Why do people have to lose things to find out what they really mean?" *- Tommy*

Of all of the musicals made during MGM's golden era, *Brigadoon* has received the most motley assortment of reviews from critics and fans alike. Director Vincente Minnelli and Gene Kelly himself felt that the entire production did not reflect what they had originally envisioned for it. Kelly was especially disappointed that the picture would not be shot on location in Scotland (due to the weather) and that, because of budget cuts, he would not be permitted to experiment with different dance sequences.

Most viewers can see the potential in *Brigadoon* that was not realized, hence, it seems like the film is only a shadow of what it could have been. However, what was made is mighty fine entertainment regardless! *Brigadoon* has a lovely magical feel to it and the staged setting actually helps create this effect rather than hinder it.

Unlike many of the characters Gene Kelly plays in musicals, Tommy is not a happy-go-lucky fellow out to have a night on the town. Instead, we see him as a confused man. He went on a hunting trip to Scotland with the hope that a vacation would clear his mind and help him to decide what he wants in life, but his brief visit to Brigadoon confuses him all the more. Prior to his trip, he was engaged to a beautiful socialite in New York City but continually put off the wedding because he was discontented with his fiancee. Once he meets Fiona, his love for her clears the fog in his heart, but

then he is torn between staying in what Jeff calls a "fairyland" or returning to "reality."

"Sometimes the things you believe in can become more real than all the things you can explain away or understand."

The film could have been developed into a light-hearted musical, much in the vein of *Seven Brides for Seven Brothers*, but then it would have risked losing its romantic mystic quality which really is the heart of the picture.

Brigadoon, which was based on the 1947 Broadway show of the same name, features a number of excellent songs by Alan Jay Lerner and Frederick Loewe including "Waitin' for my Dearie," "Almost Like Being in Love," the titular "Brigadoon," and "Heather on the Hill." The balletic dance sequences - especially "Heather on the Hill" and its reprise - are beautiful to watch, as are the more lively numbers such as "I'll Go Home with Bonnie Jean." Unfortunately, the film version cut several of Lerner and Loewe's best songs including "Come to Me, Bend to Me," "There But for You Go I," and "From This Day On."

Brigadoon went into production the same time that director Stanley Donen was planning his musical extravaganza *Seven Brides for Seven Brothers*. Metro-Goldwyn-Mayer debated whether to drop one of the two productions because they felt they could not fund both projects at once but *Seven Bride*s producer Jack Cummings insisted on continuing with the film on a cut budget. It was presumed that *Brigadoon* would be the more successful of the two films. Instead,

Seven Brides reaped nearly four times its budget, while *Brigadoon* took a loss at the box-office.

In spite of the setbacks during its production, Kelly was pleased to be starring alongside his good friend Van Johnson. Originally, actors David Wayne, Donald O'Connor, and Alec Guinness were considered for the role of Jeff instead of Johnson. Surprisingly, Oscar Levant was not considered, even though the sarcastic nature of Jeff would have suited him perfectly.

Cyd Charisse was ideally cast as Fiona; she never looked or danced better. Charisse was happy to reunite with director Vincente Minnelli whom she worked with in *The Band Wagon* just one year prior. Albert Sharpe (*Darby O'Gill and the Little People*) and Barry Jones were also perfectly cast. Hugh Laing, a ballet dancer with the New York City Ballet, was cast as Harry Beaton, the one discontented citizen of Brigadoon. Jimmy Thompson (*Singin' in the Rain*) was the handsome Charlie Dalrymple and upcoming stars George Chakiris and Stuart Whitman appear as extras.

FAMOUS AND FORGOTTEN FILMS

Brigadoon's failure at the box-office and its poor critical response marred its initial release but years later it can be seen as a highlight in MGM's output of musicals. It may not be what the director or Kelly intended it to be, but what was created was a colorful gem in itself. Aye, a bonnie good film.

Check it out!
If you like this, you'll also like.....

Seven Brides for Seven Brothers (1954)

One of MGM's most exciting musical-comedies is a tale of seven backwoods brothers and seven homespun beauties in 1850 Oregon. When Adam Pontipee's (Howard Keel) new wife Milly (Jane Powell) learns she must not only take care of her husband, but his six siblings as well, she sets out to help get all the brothers married off. With Julie Newmar, Russ Tamblyn. Songs include "When You're in Love," "Sobbin' Women," and "Spring, Spring, Spring."

*A town
...a stranger
...and the things
he does to its
people, especially
its women!*

COLUMBIA PICTURES presents

WILLIAM HOLDEN
in

WITH
KIM NOVAK

BETTY FIELD • SUSAN STRASBERG • CLIFF ROBERTSON
AND
CO-STARRING
ROSALIND RUSSELL
AS ROSEMARY

Screen play by **DANIEL TARADASH** • Based upon the play "Picnic" by **WILLIAM INGE** • Produced on the stage by **THEATRE GUILD, Inc.** and **JOSHUA LOGAN**
Directed by **JOSHUA LOGAN** • Produced by **FRED KOHLMAR**

TECHNICOLOR

THE FAMED PULITZER PRIZE PLAY...ON THE SCREEN AT LAST!

COLUMBIA PICTURES (1955)

Every year, when the flowers awaken from their dormant slumber and the magnolias begin to blossom, a familiar urge, as certain in approaching as spring itself, begins to stir within - the urge to watch *Picnic*. The film is indelibly linked in my mind with spring and, regardless of its Labor Day setting, the glow of May can be observed in every scene.

Picnic focuses on the impact a vagabond drifter makes on the womenfolk in a sleepy Kansas town during the course of one summer day. Hal Carter (William Holden) is a bum who has come to Kansas to seek out his old college roommate Alan Benson (Cliff Robertson) in the hopes that he will find him a job at one of his father's granaries.

"I gotta get someplace in this world. I just gotta."

Upon arriving fresh off of a freight train, he meets Helen (the marvelous Verna Felton) a kindly old lady who gives him some apple pie and introduces him to her neighbors, Flo Owens (Betty Field) and Flo's two daughters, the tomboy intellectual Millie (a miscast Susan Strasberg) and the bashful beauty queen Madge (Kim Novak) who is going steady with Alan. Rooming with the Owens is Rosemary Sydney (Rosalind Russell), a spinster schoolteacher.

On the surface, each of these women are satisfied and content with their lives, but within themselves they are frustrated and longing for something more. Flo Owens was deserted by her husband years ago and wants to see her daughters married off to better men than he. Rosemary Sydney, the amiable teacher always "good for a laugh" is tired of being a spinster and wants to marry Howard Bevans (Arthur O'Connell), a local shopkeeper. Millie is jealous of her older sister's beauty, while Madge thinks her mother favors Millie and is frustrated at being admired for her looks alone.

"I'm tired of just being called pretty."

When Hal arrives, his raw virility awakens in the women memories of bygone romances or, in the case of Rosemary, long-awaited for love. Every movement he makes, every muscle he flexes, sexually arouses suppressed feelings within these gals.

William Inge's Pulitzer Prize winning play "Picnic" set pulses racing to packed crowds and enjoyed a successful 477-run performance at New York's Music Box Theatre in the spring of 1953. The original cast featured Ralph Meeker as Hal, Janice Rule

as Madge, Eileen Heckart as Rosemary, and Paul Newman as Alan Benson. Incidentally, it was during the run of "Picnic" that Newman met his future wife, Joanne Woodward. Newman was also understudy for Meeker and often rehearsed his scenes with Rule's understudy, Joanne Woodward.

Columbia Pictures head Harry Cohn purchased the rights to the play for the sum of $300,000. Cohn knew that he wanted William Holden to play the lead role, but it took some coaxing to convince the 37-year-old actor that his age would not make a difference to the essence of the story. Holden reluctantly agreed and, as this was the final film in his seven picture contract with the studio, had to settle for a paltry $30,000 fee. Holden worked out at a gym to get into shape for the part and even permitted to have his chest shaven for his brawny sequences. Carroll Baker was tested for the role of Madge but it was decided that she was too childlike for the role, and Columbia's newest sensation Kim Novak was signed instead.

Susan Strasberg was making her screen debut as Millie, fresh off of a Broadway success with the lead role in "The Diary of Anne Frank." Cliff Robertson also earned his first big screen role as rich

boy Alan Benson. The role of Howard Bevens suited Arthur O'Connell so well that director Joshua Logan asked him to reprise it for the film. This launched O'Connell on a long and steady career as a Hollywood character actor.

Production on *Picnic* began on May 16, 1955, on location around Hutchinson, Kansas. The production crew on *Picnic* was top-notch and included cinematographer James Wong Howe, screenwriter Daniel Taradesh (*From Here to Eternity*) and composer George Duning. Duning revived the 1930s big-band classic "Moonglow" for the famous dance sequence and it became a hit song once again, with the dance itself becoming one of the best remembered love scenes of the 1950s.

Logan, the director of the stage play, was selected to take the helm for the film version and made an impressive directorial debut, in his subtle but compelling filming. His master strokes are in the scenes of the Labor Day picnic itself. As the camera slowly pans across the people, it unobtrusively captures vignettes straight out of a Norman Rockwell painting. There are mothers with their children, elderly couples, rowdy boys, girls warbling a duet, speeches being made, the band playing old sweet songs and marching tunes, and through it all two babies wailing. All of these elements combine to create a tapestry of American life during the early 1950s.

The principal characters are enjoying the picnic as much as anyone there and compete in all of the group events - the balloon blowing contest, ring toss, spoon catching games, and best of all, the pie eating contest, where Howard bribes a boy to push the contestant's faces into the pies.

After the festivities of the day the group lazily gather together under the shade of a grove of cottonwoods and here Hal begins to realize what it is he has been searching for in life. It is a town, a place, a home that he wants. Proud as he is of his father and his old man's boots, he does not want to fill them and be a drifter all of his life. He wants a sense of belonging, either to someone or someplace.

As evening begins to fall, everyone wanders off in pairs... Hal walks with Millie and tells her of his admiration for people with artistic talent and the love for the finer things in life; Howard and Rosemary share a bench to admire the sunset; Helen and Flo gently swing together grateful for each others company; and Alan and Madge retreat to the river's edge to discuss their future together.

"Look at the sunset. It's like the daytime didn't want to end. It's like the daytime was gonna put up a big scrap and set the world on fire to keep the nighttime from creeping on."

The picnic is a focal point for all of the principal characters and it is after the sun sets that their emotions begin to sizzle and finally ignite and explode like the Labor Day fireworks themselves.

Picnic is an extremely well-written film rich with characters of substance and at its core it is a story about the inevitability of change happening to the best laid plans. Sometimes this change is welcome and sometimes it is not.

"I got so used to things as they were. Everything was so prim. The geraniums in the window, the smell of mama's medicine, and then he walked in and it was different . He clomped around like it was still outdoors. There was a man in the house and it seemed good".

Hal is a character that we have all met at one time or another, in a variety of different forms. He represents that person that comes into your life when you were least expecting it and disrupts everything and everyone around you. He is an intruder, and whether it is for good or bad, the change these intruders bring about cannot be ignored.

Picnic opened in limited release on December 7, 1955, and was distributed nationally on February 16, 1956. It won critical acclaim, was nominated for six Academy Awards (Best Picture, Best Supporting Actor, Best Music, Best Color Art Direction and Best Editing) and grossed a whopping $6.3 million upon its release. Sixty years later, *Picnic* remains a gem of a picture and rightly deserves its place as one of the finest films of the 1950s.

Check it out!
If you like this, you'll also like.....

Peyton Place (1957)

The peaceful small town of Peyton Place in New England hides secrets and scandals, including those of residents Constance MacKenzie (Lana Turner), Michael Rossi (Lee Philips) and Selena Cross (Hope Lange). Based on Grace Metalious' popular debut novel, this lush 20th Century Fox production inspired a soap opera television series in the 1960s.

RKO PICTURES (1956)

"BEYOND A REASONABLE DOUBT"

"Put them all together they spell M-U-R-D-E-R!"

The jigsaw pieces seen on the poster to *Beyond a Reasonable Doubt* certainly capture the essence of this film - it's a puzzler. Fritz Lang directed a marvelous little thriller that keeps its audiences delighted in trying to out-guess the various twists and turns in the plot.... right up to the electrifying finale.

Sidney Blackmer portrays a publisher who is opposed to capital punishment, and so, to publicly expose the frailty of circumstantial evidence involved in most cases, he persuades his future son-in-law, novelist Dana Andrews, to be framed in the murder of a stripper - with the intention of providing proof that all the evidence used in the case was planted. However, things go dreadfully wrong and Andrews finds his life on the line when he really is accused of the crime.

"It's a weird, crazy idea, but that's the reason it intrigues me."

Beyond a Reasonable Doubt was fairly well received by critics upon its initial release and has since become a minor noir classic, in no small part due to the popularity of Fritz Lang. This film turned out to be his final Hollywood production and he left for Europe before it was even completed, leaving Gene Fowler Jr. with the task of editing it down to 80 minutes.

The film has all the elements you would expect in a noir - moody monochrome tones, a disentranced protagonist, a few seedy locales, and numerous plot twists. Even the now requisite nightclub singer is thrown in for good measure.

Joan Fontaine, who appeared in very few noirs, gives a good performance as Andrew's fiancee, distraught at the thought that her sweetheart may very well end up in the electric chair for a publicity stunt gone awry. However, it is Dana Andrew's performance that really makes the plot believable. He was going through some personal problems at the time of filming but he did not let that interfere with his performance quality. Also cast is Arthur Franz, Barbara Nichols, and Sheppard Strudwick (certainly one of the busiest character actors of the 1950s).

A man frames himself into the electric chair!

PARAMOUNT PICTURES (1957)

OMAR KHAYYAM

"Could you and I alone with Fate conspire"

In the 1940s and early 1950s colorfully costumed Arabian adventure films were all the rage. Universal studios started this string of sword and sandal spectacles in Hollywood when it released Arabian Nights, a modest box-office success starring Jon Hall. *Ali Baba and the 40 Thieves* (also with Jon Hall), *The Prince Who Was a Thief*, *Son of Ali Baba*, *A Thousand and One Nights*, and *Sinbad the Sailor* soon followed. By 1957, however, the genre was beginning to wane in popularity and it was in this year that Paramount Pictures decided to release *Omar Khayyam* starring Cornel Wilde and Debra Paget.

Omar Khayyam was a fictional biographical account of the life of the 11th century mathematician-poet who lived in Bagdad. Since very little details of his life are known, Barre Lyndon freely took the opportunity to weave a script which included sultans, thieves, intrigue, harems, and a beautiful princess. All the prime ingredients for an Arabian night fantasy.

It begins with our hero, the wise poet, discovering that his beloved is to become the Shah's newest bride. Forlorn at the thought of losing her, he obtains a position at the palace as chief astronomer to be near her, and lo! what does he discover here but schemes of betrayal stirring within the palace walls.

Cornel Wilde, who rose to fame in Hollywood for his swashbuckling films (he was a champion fencer), lacks the pizzazz that he had in his other pictures and understandably so since the role calls for a distressed lovelorn poet, not a swashbuckling hero. However, the supporting cast in *Omar Khayyam* is marvelous and more than makes up for Wilde's mild performance. Michael Rennie, always a familiar face in costumed dramas, is excellent in the role of Hasani, one of Khayyam's dear friends and later his adversary. Sebastion Cabot is also one of Khayyam's childhood friends who helps give Omar an audience with the shah, which later earns the poet the position of counselor and astronomer at the palace.

Raymond Massey, the man of one face, looks surprisingly Arabic in appearance in his role as the mighty Shah who surrounds himself with wise counselors and his two fighting sons, played by John Derek and Perry Lopez. Yma Sumac, the exotic four-octave range singer (check out her amazing performances with the Les Baxter

FAMOUS AND FORGOTTEN FILMS

Orchestra) has a brief appearance to do some warbling while Joan Taylor and Margaret Hayes round out the cast of femme fetales. Debra Paget is ravishingly beautiful as ever and was well-chosen by the Shah to be his newest wife.

Other familiar faces include Edward Platt (*Get Smart*), John Abbott, and Dick Elliott (Mayor Pike on *The Andy Griffith Show*).

The film boasts some stunning costumes by Ralph Jester who did only a handful of costume design work in films such as The Ten Commandents, Soloman and Sheba, and The Buccanneer.

William Dietrele discontinued his 27-year long Hollywood career after completing *Omar Khayyam* and it is no wonder he was dissatisfied with what he was being given. As colorful and vibrant as Khayyam is (it was filmed in VistaVision) the movie is a far cry from Dietrele's earlier biopics, such as *The Story of Louis Pasteur* and *The Life of Emile Zola*. One cannot help wondering how great it could have been had the film been approached differently. Perhaps with a different leading man, or even if it were turned into a musical.... with Howard Keel.

Nevertheless, for loyal followers of sword-and-sandal Arabian Nights flicks this is highly recommended viewing. Especially on a Saturday morning. As Khayyam would say, "A bowl of oatmeal, a jug of juice, and thou...great television set. Give me the sweet pleasures of life to while my days away".

PARAMOUNT PICTURES (1958)

"There comes a time when a man wants to change... belong to something, or maybe someone."

The pirate and privateer Jean Lafitte had warehouses of stolen loot, a beautiful house on the private island in Barataria Bay, and freedom to do as he pleased, but he lacked respect from the one woman he loved, Annette Claiborne. This woman instills in him a love for the still infant American nation strong enough to make him surrender his pirating ways and seek to become a citizen. But first he must prove to Governor Claiborne, Annette's father, that he is not in league with the British who are about to send thousands of troops into Louisiana to squash General Andrew Jackson's defense of the territory.

In 1956, director Cecil B. DeMille had found great success with the remake of his silent film *The Ten Commandments*, and so he undertook another remake of a favorite film of his, *The Buccaneer*, first made in 1938 with Fredric March in the lead. During the making of *The Ten Commandments*, DeMille had suffered a heart attack but he had sufficiently recovered to believe that he was capable of undertaking another epic production. He was wrong. Shortly after the initial planning of *The Buccaneer*, DeMille realized that his health would not permit him to make the film and so he passed the directorial wand to his son-in-law, Anthony Quinn.

Quinn had never directed a feature film but was willing to give it a try with his father-in-law helping to guide the production. This was the primary reason DeMille had selected Quinn - in order to have full control of the final production. Both came to regret this decision. DeMille was displeased with the film that Quinn had helmed and made editing changes to it before its release that Quinn did not like.

Just why Cecil B. DeMille and Anthony Quinn were dissatisfied with the final result is difficult to fathom. While it is true that *The Buccaneer* lacks the compelling drama of *The Ten Commandments*, the film is colorful, entertaining, and does pack quite a bit of adventure into its 119-minute runtime. The battle scene at the end of the film is particularly thrilling with the bagpiping British troops appearing from the fog (a scene that Walt Disney's *Bedknobs and Broomsticks* would later echo).

Unfortunately, the script to *The Buccaneer*, based upon the 1938 film, has mere threads of real history in its plot. Instead, the screenwriters (Jesse Lasky Jr., Berenice Mosk) fashioned a script that captures merely the flavor of the era and its setting. You can't ask for everything.

Yul Brynner, sporting a rare mop of hair, gives a convincing portrayal of the good-hearted privateer longing for a place to anchor. Lafitte is a likable and sympathetic character, as is his companion General Dominique You, played by Charles Boyer. "Of all the men in the world, I never wanted to fail you," Lafitte tells the General in a poignant scene when Lafitte realizes that his friendship with the General may be the price he has to pay for American citizenship.

Charlton Heston, who is always a pleasure to watch, gives a powerful performance as General Andrew Jackson, reprising a role that he had played in *The President's Lady* (1953). Taking care of "Old Ironface" Jackson, making sure that he drinks his hot milk every night, is Mr. Peavy, played by the great character actor Henry Hull.

The ladies are equally engaging. Inger Stevens, that icy blonde from Sweden, stars as the beautiful Annette Claiborne. She is in love with the pirate and is willing to surrender her status as a Southern society belle to sail off with him into the open sea. The marvelous Claire Bloom plays Bonnie Brown, a feisty tomboy who wants Lafitte as well. But her love is so deep she would rather see him wed to Ms. Claiborne than be with her.

"You're a fool! She's everything you ever loved and fought for. You gave up everything you had, everything you are. Jean, even I don't want to see you lose her now."

Also in the cast is E.G. Marshall, Lorne Greene, Ted de Corsia, Douglass Dumbrille, and Fran Jeffries.

FAMOUS AND FORGOTTEN FILMS

At the box-office, *The Buccaneer* did poorly, bringing in only $3 million dollars in revenue, not even recuperating its $5 million dollar budget. When discussing the films of Cecil B. DeMille, *The Buccaneer* is rarely mentioned, even though his handiwork is clearly evident in many of the scenes. DeMille is also credited at the beginning of the film before the titles appear. But perhaps modern critics consider the production too run-of-DeMille to be even mentioned among his works.

Sinbad attacks the fire-breathing dragon—as DYNAMATION brings you nostril-close to this suddenly *real* monster!
Cyclops roast Sinbad's men — as DYNAMATION brings you the 1001 thrills of fiction's most famed argosy!
DYNAMATION, fabulous new process, was invented by artist-genius Ray Harryhausen, four of whose imaginative drawings based on sensational "Sinbad" scenes are reproduced here. DYNAMATION makes the fantastic fantastically *real!*
All-out rout of Sinbad's band — as DYNAMATION makes the gruesome Giant even more gigantic!
Sinbad's duel-to-the-death with a living Skeleton —as DYNAMATION makes the legendary *real!*
THE 7th VOYAGE OF SINBAD
DYNAMATION
Technicolor®
STARRING
KERWIN MATHEWS · KATHRYN GRANT · CO-STARRING RICHARD EYER AS THE GENIE · WITH TORIN THATCHER
WRITTEN BY KENNETH KOLB · VISUAL EFFECTS CREATED BY RAY HARRYHAUSEN · PRODUCED BY CHARLES H. SCHNEER · DIRECTED BY NATHAN JURAN · A MORNINGSIDE PRODUCTION · A COLUMBIA PICTURE

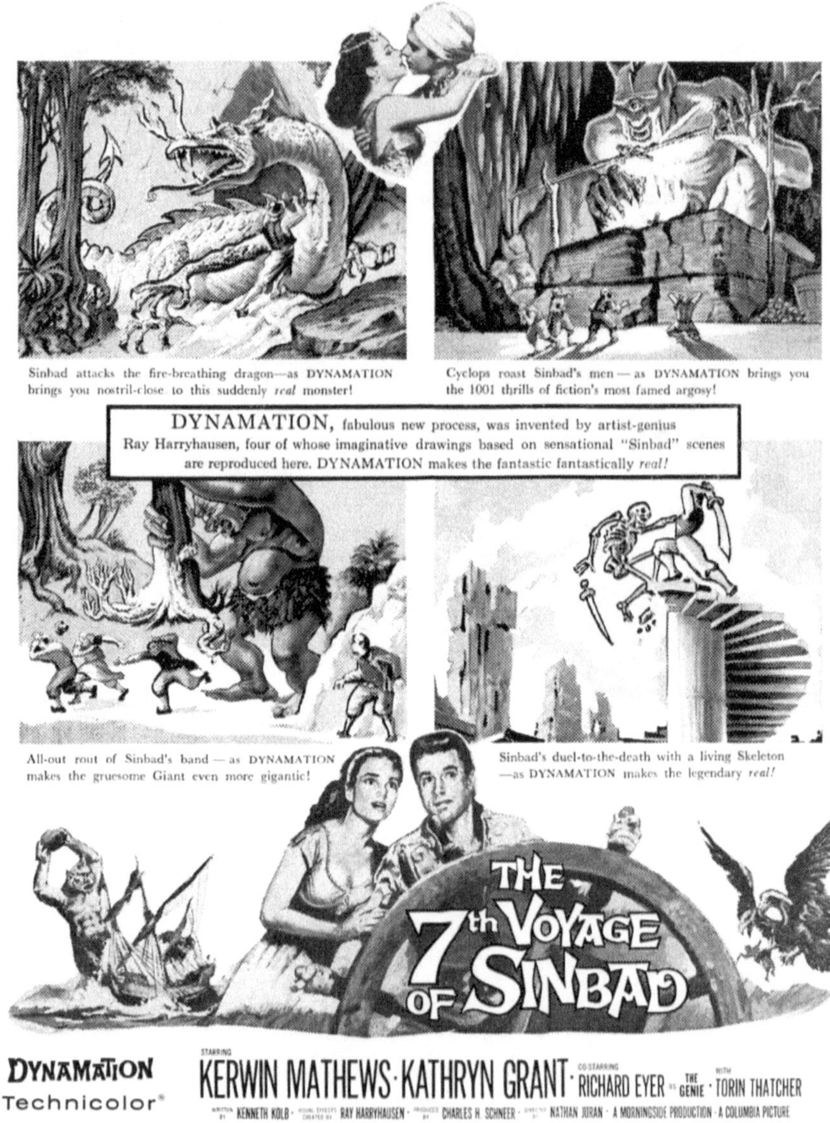

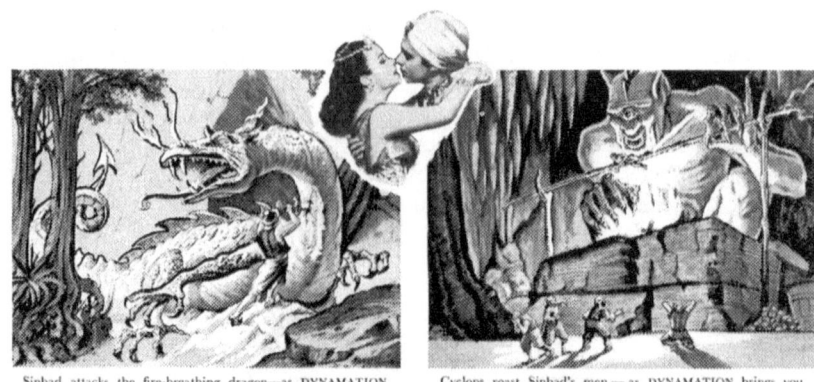

COLUMBIA PICTURES (1958)

THE 7th VOYAGE OF SINBAD

"From the land beyond beyond, from the world past hope and fear, I bid you Genie now appear!"

Legendary adventurer Sinbad the Sailor (Kerwin Mathews) lands on the island of Colossa for provisions when he en-counters and helps rescue the magician Sokurah (Torin Thatcher) who is fleeing from the giant cyclops on the island. After their boat is overturned in the escape, Sokurah loses the magic lamp he was carrying which is then retrieved by the cyclops. The conniving magician attempts to bribe Sinbad to return to the island for the lamp but to no avail and so he shrinks Princess Parisa (Kathryn Grant), Sinbad's betrothed, to the size of a doll. The potion to restore her to her normal size requires the shell of a bird's egg that can only be found on Colossa. With no choice before him, Sinbad agrees to make the journey back to Colossa where he must fight the cyclops and battle with Sokurah's magic to save the princess.

The 7th Voyage of Sinbad was producer Charles Schneer's fourth film collaboration with special effects artist Ray Harryhausen and it features some of Harryhausen's finest stop-motion animation, including the first appearance of his famous fighting skeleton figure. This film was also notable for being the first fantasy film that Harryhausen worked on, having previously created creatures for science-fiction films such as *20 Million Miles to Earth* (1957).

In *Sinbad*, our hero encounters a wide array of beasts that he must contend with. There is the giant man-eating cyclops, the two-headed roc, the fighting skeleton, and the fierce guardian dragon Taro, all of which were created by Harryhausen in the newly-dubbed Dynamation process.

Charles Schneer pulled out all the stops with *The 7th Voyage of Sinbad* and it had the largest budget of any of his films to date - $650,000. It took Harryhausen eleven months to create the stop-motion effects alone, in which time the cast was filming the live-action sequences under the capable hand of director Nathan Juran. Location filming took place in sunny Spain, a locale that would be used in most of Schneer's subsequent fantasy films.

FAMOUS AND FORGOTTEN FILMS

The brilliant composer Bernard Herrmann (a favorite of Alfred Hitchcock) was called in to compose the score for *The 7th Voyage of Sinbad* and what he created was a marvelous and imaginative composition that conjures up ancient Arabia in its musical strains. He teamed up with Charles Schneer and Ray Harryhausen again to create the music for *Mysterious Island* (1961) and *Jason and the Argonauts* (1963).

Kerwin Mathews plays our Arabian hero Captain Sinbad and he does a wonderful job with the part. His loyal companion is Harufa, portrayed by Alfred Brown, and his beloved Princess Parisa is played by pretty Kathryn Grant. Child-actor Richard Eyer also gives a good performance as the echo-voiced genie, Barani. Being a loyal albeit reluctant genie, no matter what deed he is asked to perform Barani does his best to accomplish, meekly answering, "I shall try, o master, I shall try."

Also in the cast is the great character actor Torin Thatcher who redefined the word villain with his performance of the devious magician Sokurah. He desperately wants the genie's lamp and would willingly trade all the treasure hoarded by the cyclops' in place of that lamp, knowing full well the power it wields.

The 7th Voyage of Sinbad would be classified as juvenile fare, but it really does entertain no matter what age you are. From its opening sequence at sea to its finale, it features non-stop action. The film was very popular at the box office earning over $3 million in receipts and inspiring Harryhausen to pursue more fantasy films, but it would not be until 1973 that audiences would see another Sinbad film - *The Golden Voyage of Sinbad*, which was later followed by the equally entertaining *Sinbad and the Eye of the Tiger* (1977).

Check it out!
If you like this, you'll also like.....

Jack the Giant Killer (1962)

After rescuing the beautiful Princess Elaine, farmboy-turned-knight Jack is charged by the king to escort her to safety and protect her from the minions of an evil wizard. Great animated creatures-- dragons, sea monsters, and, of course, a giant or two--highlight this fine fantasy/adventure in the tradition of the "Sinbad" films. Kerwin Mathews, Judi Meredith, and Torin Thatcher star.

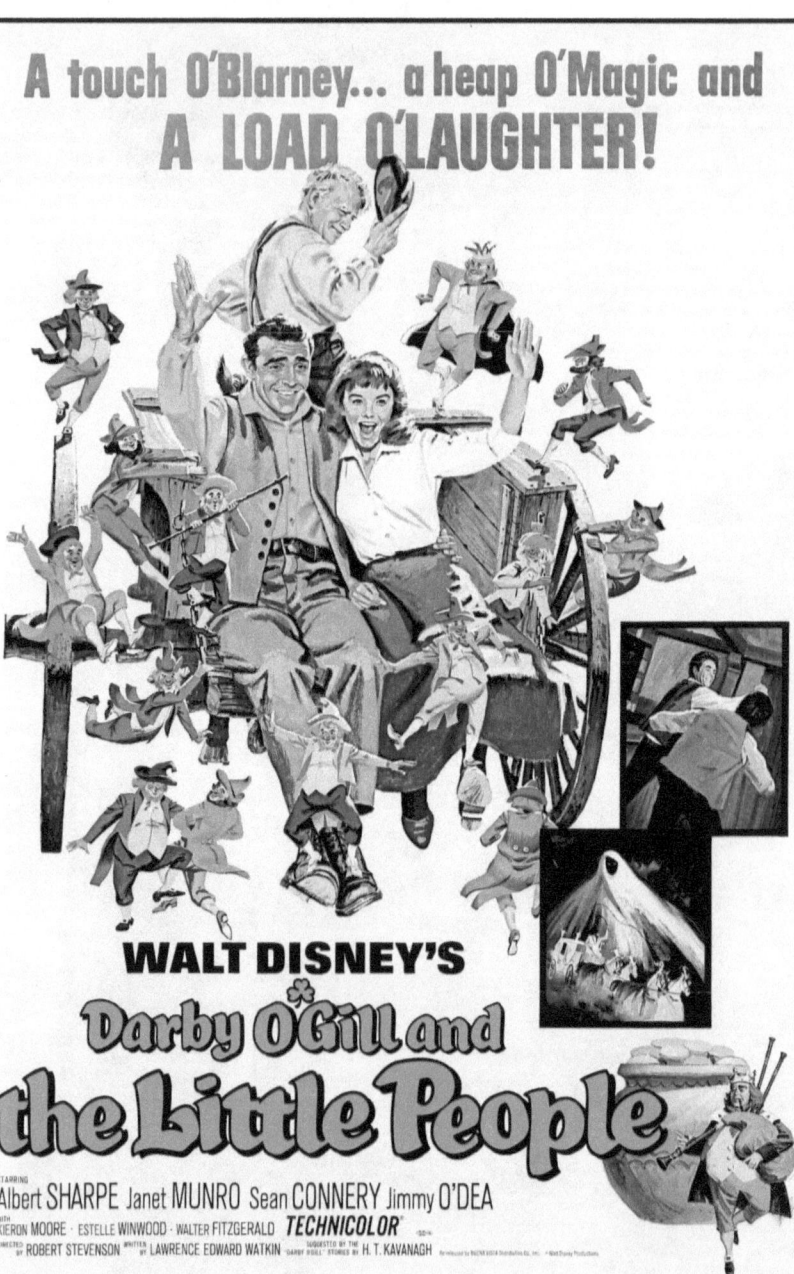

WALT DISNEY STUDIOS (1959)

WALT DISNEY'S
Darby O'Gill
and the Little People

"Three wishes I'll grant ye, great wishes an' small! But you wish a fourth and you'll lose them all!"

Darby O'Gill is a wily old codger, but even with all his experience he canno' match wits with the king of the leprechauns, King O'Brien himself. On a spooky moonlit night in Ireland, Darby falls down a well on Fairy Mountain and comes face to face with the king and his band of little people. Darby manages to capture O'Brien and then demands of him his rightful three wishes....one naturally being the proverbial pot o'gold. But the King has learned more than a few tricks over the course of five thousand years and Darby finds that he has to keep a bridle on his tongue in order to hold onto his wishes.

Darby O'Gill and the Little People is one of the best live-action films that the Walt Disney Studios released during the 1950s, featuring an amusing script full of Irish wit, engaging actors, a heap o'magical effects and legions of little people.

Walt Disney had his hand in all of the films his studio released, but he felt a special attachment to this project. Disney read the Darby O'Gill stories by H.T. Kavanagh in the mid-1940s and decided at that time to create a film based on them. He saw Albert Sharpe performing on stage in "Finian's Rainbow" and knew then and there that he was the man to portray Darby.

Albert Sharpe, a true Irishman, was indeed marvelous as Darby, but it was Jimmy O'Dea, as King Brian of Knocknasheega, who stole every scene he was in. Faith, this wee little man had a sparkle about him and, if you happen to be quick enough to capture a leprechaun yourself, surely he would resemble O'Dea in more ways than one.

"Oh, she is my dear, my darlin' one, her eyes so sparklin' full of fun....no other, no other, can match the likes of her!"

Janet Munro, as Darby O'Gill's daughter Katie, was such a winsome delight that Disney signed her to a contract and she went on to make *The Third Man on the Mountain* (1959) and *Swiss Family Robinson* (1960) for the studio. And, your eyes be not deceiving you, there indeed be a young Sean Connery who portrays Michael McBride, the strapping lad who is replacing Darby as the new caretaker of Lord Fitzpatrick's manor.

FAMOUS AND FORGOTTEN FILMS

The beautiful scenery of Ireland was created through matte backdrops painted by Peter Ellenshaw, which made the film a visual delight. The Emerald Isle never looked so green as it did in Ellenshaw's paintings. Eustace Lycett, Disney's resident wizard of magic, wielded his wand as well to create some stunning effects including the truly terrifying Coiste-bodhar and the glowing Banshee.

"It's the Coiste-bodhar! The death coach!"

To help promote the film on television, Walt Disney filmed a short entitled "I Captured the King of the Leprechauns" in which Walt travels to Ireland to talk with Darby about the proper method of capturing a leprechaun and how he was able to film the little folk during their festive dancing. Forsooth, they were not seen on camera again for many many years.

Alas, upon its release *Darby O'Gill and the Little People* was not the big box-office attraction that Disney hoped it would be and that disappointed him sorely. However, over the years it has been recognized for being the grand film that it is and has grown a large following of fans. Watching this beloved classic is now a St. Patrick's Day tradition in many a home.

NUGGET REVIEWS

"There's gold in them thar films!"

MERRILL'S MERAUDERS (1962) *14k*

General Frank Merrill takes 3,000 infantry volunteers through some of the thickest jungle of Burma to help relieve the British troops by taking the airstrip at Myitkyina. *Jeff Chandler, Ty Hardin, Andrew Duggan, Claude Akins, Peter Brown, John Hoyt. Directed by Samuel Fuller, Warner Brothers.*

This film is full of actors who look like other actors... Jeff Chandler reminded me of Gregory Peck here, Ty Hardin of Jeffrey Hunter, and Peter Brown of Stephen Boyd. John Hoyt was excellent as General Stillwell and the location shots were beautiful but other than that this is a standard war film. It seems to build up to a climax which, disappointingly, never happens.

THE GLASS SLIPPER (1955) *Elct.*

The rebellious "Ella" falls in love with a cook's son, not realizing that he is actually the Duke's son....her very own Prince Charming. *Leslie Caron, Michael Wilding, Elsa Lanchester, Keenan Wynn, Amanda Blake. MGM Pictures. Directed by Charles Walters.*

This was another case of MGM thinking they could replicate a success (1953's Lili) by following it up with a similarly themed film. Helen Deutsch, who had written the screenplay

THE LATE GEORGE APLEY (1947) *18k*

A warm and humorous look at the life of one George Apley, a 100% proof Bostonian - during the first decade of the 20th century, and the circumstances leading up to his children's marriages. *Ronald Colman, Peggy Cummins, Edna Best, Richard Haydn, Richard Ney, Mildred Natwick. Directed by Joseph Mankiewicz. 20th Century Fox.*

This film was absolutely delightful. It tickled me pink....but then I'm a great fan of Richard Haydn and dry humor. This plays out much like an Oscar Wilde comedy. Ronald Colman is excellent in his role as stuff-shirted George Apley, as is the rest of the cast.

to Lili, penned this rather silly re-telling of the Cinderella fairy tale. The elements that made the original fairy tale so endearing were removed. Cinderella is no longer a sweet-natured woman who bears her toilsome life with patience. Instead, she is "Ella", a tomboyish waif who sulks around wishing she were dead. No doubt Deutsch intended to add a touch of 1950s realism (and teenage rebel behavior) to the character, but in doing so she made the romance that springs between her and Prince Charming completely unbelievable.

COLUMBIA PICTURES (1959)

Edge Of Eternity

Savage suspense spans the granite gorge!

So heralds the poster for *Edge of Eternity*, a taut mystery thriller set in the midst of a decaying mining town in Arizona in the late 1950s.

The opening scene plays out like an episode of the television series *Perry Mason*: An elderly businessman parks his car at the very edge of the Grand Canyon. He brings out a pair of binoculars and, just as he is beginning to look through them at something below, a large burly younger man jumps from behind the rocks and attacks him. The two wrestle, but it is the younger man who topples off the cliff to his death.

Later, Deputy Sheriff Les Martin (Cornel Wilde) receives a phone call from Eli, the watchman of a closed-down gold mine. The businessman is in his office, sputtering something incoherently. Les is on his way to the mine when he witnesses a speeding driver and

takes off in pursuit of it. The driver is Janice Kendon (Victoria Shaw), the daughter of the mine's owner. He writes her a ticket, but in the time he spent doing so, the businessman is murdered! This begins a strange series of killings, all committed in very different ways. The community leaders want action and Les and his boss, Sheriff Edwards (Edgar Buchanan), find themselves under increasing pressure to solve the crimes.

Edge of Eternity is not a well-known title, even among Cornel Wilde fans, yet it is an engrossing little thriller and deserves to be more frequently aired on television. The story seems like a plot from a 1970s made-for-television mystery, but thankfully it was given a much better treatment here by director Don Siegel (*Invasion of the Body Snatchers, Dirty Harry*).

This Columbia Pictures release was filmed in Eastmancolor in Arizona with the vast panoramic landscape of the Grand Canyon providing a parched yet picturesque backdrop to Knut Swenson and Richard Collins' noir-style screenplay, which keeps you guessing to the very end who the killer may be.

Red herrings abound in the form of suspicious glances and double-entendre dialogue from supposedly trustworthy characters; the number one suspects being Janice's brother Bob Kendon (Rian Garrick) and Sheriff Edwards himself, admirably played by Edgar Buchanan.

Buchanan played in a wide array of films in a career that spanned nearly 35 years. Most of his characters were lovable rascals with a streak of mischief in them, a role epitomized in Uncle Joe in the long-running *Petticoat Junction* series. He was also a familiar face in westerns, one of the most famous being *Shane* (1953), where he played homesteader Fred Lewis. Yet, Buchanan was much more capable an actor than his Uncle Joe character would have you believe.

Sheriff Edwards appears to be such a likable guy. Les is indebted to him for giving him a second chance after a botched murder investigation wrecked his career as a policeman. He not only trusts him but sees Edwards as a father figure, a man he can lean on for support and advice, both personally and professionally. Edwards is just an all-around likable fellow. But gosh, he says so many little things that get you wondering whether Les' trust in him is not misplaced. Credit for his character being so ambiguous could go to the screenwriters but I believe Buchanan's portrayal of Sheriff Edwards is what really makes this work.

Reliable Cornel Wilde also gives a good performance. For years he starred in swashbucklers and other period films, always playing a hero with clean morals. In *Edge of Eternity*, he plays a knight-in-shining-armor as well, but one of the laid-back modest variety, garbed in the uniform of a kindly deputy. Les takes a fancy to the rich and reckless Janice and, not surprisingly, he quickly wins her heart. In the climactic finale, he risks his life for her fighting with the killer in a cable car suspended high atop the Grand Canyon. This nail-biting scene is what *Edge of Eternity* is best known for and it is an excellent cap-off to a fine mystery thriller.

Also in the cast are Alexander Lockwood as Janice's father, Mickey Shaughnessy as a bartender, Tom Fadden, and Jack Elam in a brief role.

WALT DISNEY PICTURES (1959)

WALT DISNEY'S the SHAGGY DOG

In the mid-1950s, Walt Disney gave ABC network their very first full-hour western television program - *Davy Crockett*. The series was such a success that the network soon launched many other similar series such as *Maverick*, *Wyatt Earp*, and *Lawman*. These westerns brought ABC so much income that in 1957, when Walt Disney approached them with a fresh idea for a sitcom (sans the gun belts and tumbleweed) they turned him away. This minor detail didn't bother Mr.Disney in the least since he turned the material that he had offered ABC into a feature film release. *The Shaggy Dog* became one of the top-grossing films of 1959 earning $9,000,000 at the box-office and out-performing *The Diary of Anne Frank* and *North by Northwest*. That's something to bark about.

What made this low-budget comedy such a smashing hit? For one thing, it was a novelty. After a decade of musicals, crime dramas, spectacles, and method-acting melodramas, here was a little film that played out like a television series, a *Leave it to Beaver* versus Enemy Agents. It was unique. It was fun. And above all, it was great family entertainment. Walt knew how to appeal to all ages and

The Shaggy Dog provided entertainment and humor for the young and old alike. It was filled with excitement, clever dialogue, and plenty of visual gags. The studio went on to recycle many of these gags in their recurring films.

Unlike the other box-office hits of 1959, *The Shaggy Dog* did not have any moments of great splendor, instead it leisurely followed the story line only to stop occasionally to wittily comment on the social status at the time or sprinkle gentle humor. Writer Bill Walsh penned the amusing screenplay based on the 1930 novel, "The Hound of Florence", by Austrian author Felix Salten *(Bambi)*.

The Shaggy Dog follows the adventures of a junior scientist who accidentally recites an ancient Borgia curse that releases a 400-year-old shape-shifting spell. With the magical words "In Canis Corpore Transmuto," Wilby Daniels transforms himself into a big, shaggy dog - a Bratislavian sheepdog to be precise - belonging to the new neighbors on the block. It is while being in the four-footed state that Wilby overhears a plot to steal a secret missile plan at the nearby air base. It's Shaggy to the rescue then as he tries to convince his father, and the local authorities, that Continental spies are at work in the neighborhood!

"In Canis Corpore Transmuto...In Canis Corpore Transmuto.... it's a dosy do and awaaaay we go!"

The Shaggy Dog boasted a fine cast of young players, all of whom would come to be associated with the Walt Disney Studios. Tim Considine took a radical turn from his wholesome *Spin and Marty* role to play Wilby's scheming friend Buzz. At the expense of his good ol' pal, he whizzes around in his hot-rod wooing the most eligible girls in town. One of these girls just happens to be Allison, played by Annette Funicello in a brief part, her first film appearance. She is soon replaced as Girl No. 1 when sophisticated Franceska Andrassy (Roberta Shore) moves in with her father in the big Victorian manor across the street. If this street looks familiar, it is because it is the Universal cul-se-sac featured in *The Munsters, The Burbs* and *Leave it To Beaver*.

Tommy Kirk proves to be in top form as Wilby Daniels. Although he made many more films with Walt Disney during the 1960s, none of his roles would be as appealing as Wilby. Tagging along as a mischievous helpmate is his little brother Moochie, naturally played by Mickey Mouse Club "Moochie" himself - Kevin Corcoran. Moochie doesn't display much surprise when he discovers his brother is a dog, but rather jumps at the notion of having a pet playmate to take on walks and throw sticks to. Corcoran later went on to become a producer with the Walt Disney studios in the 1970s and 1980s.

Unlike the childish, bumbling crooks seen throughout the Walt Disney productions of the 1990s, *The Shaggy Dog* featured some pretty normal rough-and-tough criminals (played by Anthony Scourby and Jacques Aubuchon), although in this flick they are spies and quite debonair to look at. In fact, they are so suave that our damsel-in-distress does not even realize they are up to no good until after they kidnap her. Our devious villains conjure up images of the sophisticated foils that were so popular in series of the 1940s, such as those seen in *Sherlock Holmes, Michael Shayne,* or *The Three Stooges* shorts. These criminals are upstanding citizens loaded with wealth which they love to lavish on their collections of fine art and furniture. No one in the community would even dare consider them to be enemies of the state.

Fred MacMurray had been making films covering every possible genre since he began his career back in 1929. After making a number of mediocre pictures during the 1950s, Disney asked Fred if he would be willing to try his hand at comedy once again. *The*

Shaggy Dog marked the beginning of a seven picture association he had with Walt Disney Studios. In the film, MacMurray plays a retired mailman and the father of our two leading lads. He has an allergic reaction to dogs that makes him despise the mere mention of their name and prompts him to bring out his trusty double-barreled shotgun from the hall closet.

"You know that dog thing is all in your mind"

"All in my mind?! I itch, my sinuses are bloating up, my throat is constricting so that I can hardly breath, those old Pekingese wounds on my ankle are throbbing like bongo drums...and you say it's all in my mind!"

One of Fred's best scenes involved him trying to convince the head of security at the missile plant that his son is a dog. Variety magazine noted, "It's a pleasure to see such a master of timing and emphasis as Fred MacMurray back in comedy again, even though he is somewhat limited in his material. Where he has a good line, he shows that he has few peers in this special field of comedy".

Playing his wife is the lovely Jean Hagen, another gal who had her share of duds before snagging this wholesome part. Cecil Kellaway, Paul Frees (a legendary voice-over actor for Walt Disney Studios), Forest Lewis and Gordon Jones rounded out the great cast, but let's not forget the film's star player - the shaggy dog. "Chiffon" was in fact Sammy's Shadow, a talented pooch belonging to a California State Division of Highways clerk. He had an illustrious pedigree and, after enrolling in William Koehler's obedience training classes at the age of 4 months, he joined the Allied Movie Dogs firm and landed this wild and woolly part. Twenty sheepdogs had been tested for the part but Koehler knew he had a winner with Sammy and it is truly the dog performing all of the stunts seen in the film (except for one talking sequence where a hand puppet was used). Sammy went on to win the 1960 PATSY (Picture Animal Top Star of the Year) award for his performance in *The Shaggy Dog*.

The Shaggy Dog has held up well over time, which is a testament to the enduring strength of a simple story told well. It is also notable for instigating important changes within Disney's production outlook for the coming decades. It was the first film to use animated title sequences and the picture's success told the studio that live-action comedy films were a profitable venture not to be overlooked. Unfortunately, they held to its "formula" so closely that many of the later Disney productions lacked novelty.

THE SHAGGY D.A. (1976)

Wilby Daniels, now all grown up and running for district attorney, finds himself once again turning into a shaggy dog at inopportune moments. Dean Jones, Suzanne Pleshette and Tim Conway star.

UNIVERSAL PICTURES (1961)

A MAJORITY of ONE

"Any man more right than his neighbors constitutes a majority of one"

Leonard Spigelgass' poignant story of racial prejudice, *A Majority of One*, focuses on emphasizing the truth of the above quotation as well as teaching a gentle and humorous lesson on the folly of judging others by their ethnicity and not by their hearts. It is a story of a cross-cultural romance between two widows – Mrs. Jacoby, a Jewish Brooklynite (superbly played by Rosiland Russell) and Mr. Asano (Alec Guinness), a Japanese industrialist.

Mrs. Jacoby spent most of her life in Flatbush and loves the neighborhood and her apartment dearly. Her daughter Alice

(Madlyn Rhue) and diplomat son-in-law Jerry (Ray Danton) worry about "Mama" living on her own while they spend years at a time in foreign nations moving wherever Jerry's position takes them. Mrs. Jacoby is not getting any younger and, as her neighbor Mrs. Ruben blatantly points out, the neighborhood is changing and "that element is moving in"....a statement which brings up a conversation that sets the tone for the film:

"What element, Mrs. Ruben?" (Jerry)

"You know..colored, Puerto Ricans..."

"Really? I seem to remember in this very neighborhood not so long ago they didn't allow Jews."

"What does one have to do with the other?"

"Everything. The only way to stop prejudice is to stop it in yourself".

When Jerry receives his new assignment, Alice pleads with Mama to come with them. "But you haven't said where"..."Japan, Mama." Japan! Mrs. Jacoby lost her only son in combat in Japan during WWII and the memory – the hatred – is still painfully fresh. However, for love of her children, she reluctantly agrees to follow, and so they're off across the sea to the Land of the Rising Sun. En route on the voyage they meet Mr. Asano, a Japanese millionaire industrialist who will not only play a pivotal role in an upcoming international trade conference that Jerry will take part in, but will change Mrs. Jacoby's feelings

MRS. JACOBY (ROSALIND RUSSELL) ON SHIPBOARD—
DAUGHTER MADLYN RHUE AND SON-IN-LAW RAY DANTON

IN WESTERN CLOTHES, THE BROOKLYN WIDOW AND
THE JAPANESE WIDOWER VISIT ON A SUNNY DECK

IN EASTERN DRESS AND IN THE JAPANESE HOME OF
THE ORIENTAL TYCOON, THEY LOOK QUITE DIFFERENT

toward the Japanese in a remarkable way.

A Majority of One was penned by Spigelgass in 1958 and debuted on Broadway on February 16, 1959, starring Gertrude Berg and Sir Cedric Hardwicke. It played for 556 performances and was a critical and box-office success. It was nominated for four Tony awards (Berg won for Best Actress).

Jack Warner at Warner Bros. purchased the film rights to the comedy in 1960 for the princely sum of $500,000 and approached Rosalind Russell for the starring role. Russell was aghast. "You've been drinking," she told Warner according to her 1977 autobiography *Life is a Banquet.* "What would I be doing playing a Jewish lady from Brooklyn? I'm a little Irish girl from Waterbury, Connecticut. Use Gertrude Berg, it's her part." Warner insisted however, refusing to cast Berg since she made a disastrous film at Paramount years earlier. It was not until he suggested that Alec Guinness could be her co-star that Russell reconsidered. "Well, that's another cup of chicken soup," she told him. "I'll think about that little item."

When she approached Alec Guinness with the idea he said, "I want the dollars, so if you'll do it, I'll do it." To which Russell replied, "I want to work with you, so if you'll do it, I'll do it."

So they did it. And they couldn't have been a more delightful combination. Russell shines in her role as the Jewish widow, Bertha

Jacoby. With just the right amount of mamish chochmeh she dispenses bits of neighborly advice – and Smith Brothers cough drops - to all she comes in contact with. She handles herself and her children with respect, but upon occasion, when they overstep their boundaries, she can be firm and immovable.

Guinness was touching and endearing and portrayed Mr. Asano with a graceful maturity befitting a Japanese gentleman of illustrious birth. However, in spite of the heavy makeup and authenticity he gave to his role (he spent ten days in Japan prior to filming taking a crash course in Japanese culture), many viewers felt a Japanese actor was called for. Perhaps because a Caucasian portrayed the role on Broadway (interracial romance was a scandalous subject at the time and was dealt with by using English actors in the roles of Asians), or because the studio wanted top drawing names, Japanese actors such as Sessue Hayakawa were overlooked.

Marc Marno and Mae Questel were plucked from the Broadway production for supporting roles to round out a cast which also included Frank Wilcox, Francis De Sales and Alan Mowbray.

A Majority of One is a humorous blending of schmaltz and saki and went on to win three Golden Globes for Best Picture, Best Actress (Russell) and Best Film Promoting International Understanding. How did it win that last award? Because all cultures are different, the movie tells us, but those differences are just superficial. As they become acquainted, Mr. Asano and Mrs. Jacoby mention aspects of their respective cultures that, at first, seem different but after comparison are revealed to be relatively the same.

For example, Japanese people worship in shrines; Jewish people worship by blessing Sabbath candles – ultimately, "God's house is God's house," as Mrs. Jacoby says after being invited to a Japanese shrine. Japanese people eat raw fish; Jewish people eat gefilte fish. Japanese people toast with "Kanpai" and Jews say "L'Chaim."

Jews put up with a lot: "Whatever comes into your life, you take." So do Japanese: "You transcend. It's the philosophy of the Zen Buddhists." ..."You mean, if you have tsouris – trouble – you come out of it a better person for having lived through it." ...."Obviously you have studied Zen Buddhism, Mrs. Jacoby!"

In addition to emphasizing the importance of embracing other nationalities "whether they are white, black, pink or purple" the more subtle lessons of forgiveness and tolerance are taught, lessons which Mrs. Jacoby - and her children - needed to be taught. When he first makes her acquaintance, Mr. Asano approaches Mrs. Jacoby to inquire why she is so cold towards him. After telling him that her son was killed in action by the Japanese, he explains that he, personally, did not want war nor did anyone he knew, and that he lost both his son and daughter in Hiroshima. Mrs. Jacoby then realizes that he's had a cupful in life too and hatred quickly dispels into kinsmanship. As the voyage progresses they find each other to be the most pleasant of companions, with Mr. Asano particularly drawn to Mrs. Jacoby's warmth and friendship.

Later, as Mama considers the proposition of "crossing over the bridge" with Mr. Asano, she finds she must first deal with the prejudism right in her own family. In the first half of the drama we perceive Mrs. Jacoby to be old-fashioned and set in her customs while her children are shown to be adaptable and open to new viewpoints and new changes. However, the tables turn midway through and we find that it is Mrs. Jacoby's daughter and husband who are narrow-minded. The words Jerry spoke in Brooklyn echo back to him when he faces the prospect of Mama and Mr. Asano's impending courtship... "If you want to stop prejudice you must first stop it in yourself". He must come to learn that being friendly and welcoming should not be a diplomatic "front of face" but stem from a sincere consideration for others.

A Majority of One is as relevant today as it was when it was first released in 1961. The film is a hidden gem, a truly entertaining foreign affair, completely unique and as lovely as cherry blossoms in spring; it is sure to bring shtick naches to those who take the time to watch the film.

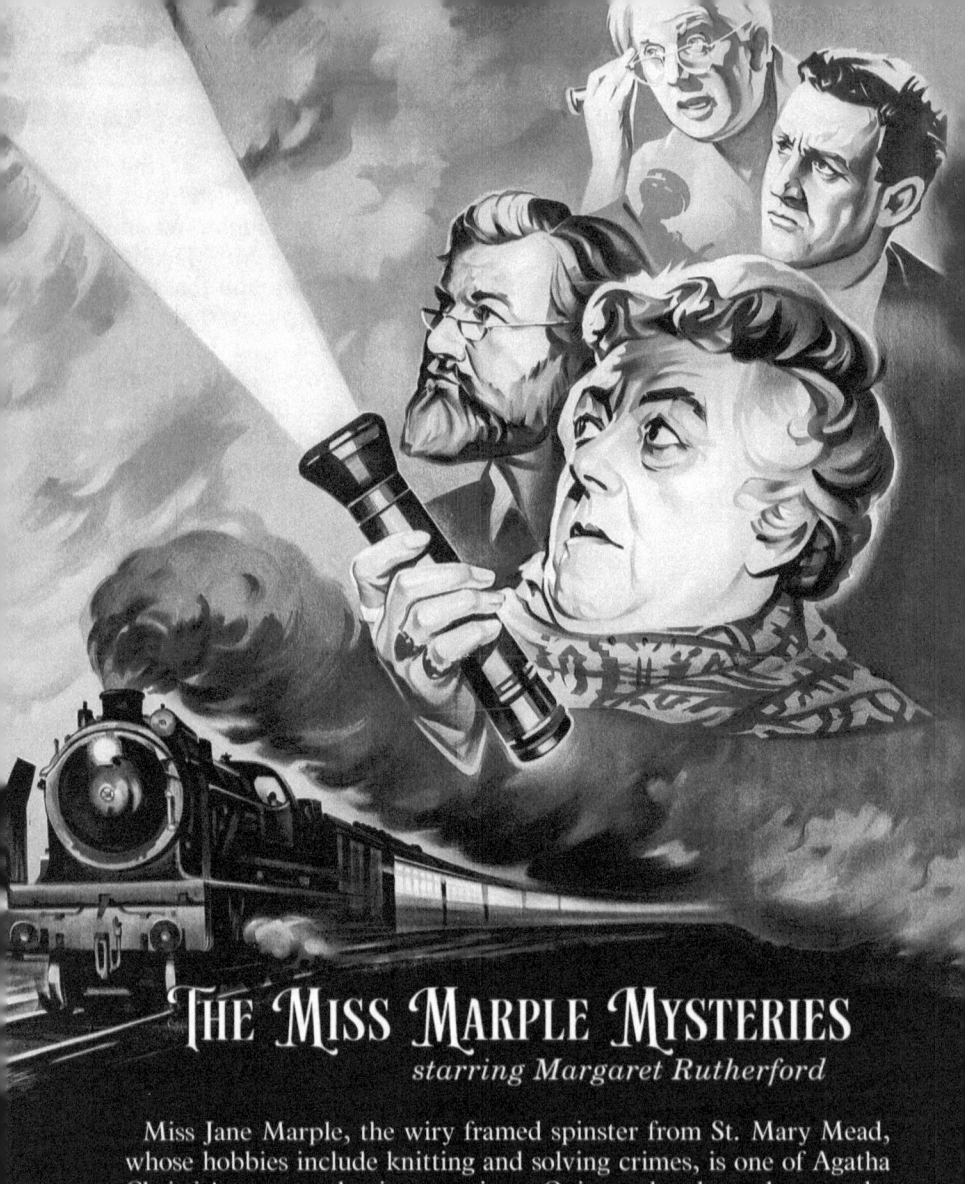

THE MISS MARPLE MYSTERIES
starring Margaret Rutherford

Miss Jane Marple, the wiry framed spinster from St. Mary Mead, whose hobbies include knitting and solving crimes, is one of Agatha Christie's most endearing creations. Quiet and sedate, she was the complete opposite of Hercule Poirot, Christie's very own Sherlock Holmes, but went on to become the star of the show in twelve novels and thirty-two short stories between 1926 and 1976.

FAMOUS AND FORGOTTEN FILMS

It is no wonder then that Metro-Goldwyn-Mayer saw an ideal character to bring to the screen. In early 1960 the studio purchased the rights to most of the author's stories for the comely sum of three million dollars in the hopes of creating a television series around the lovable sleuth. When this idea fell through, they set their sights on securing 72-year-old Margaret Rutherford, one of Great Britain's most beloved character actresses to play the part in a film version of one of Miss Marple's most entertaining novels, "4:50 from Paddington".

Agatha Christie had disapproved of this casting from the start. She had modeled Miss Marple after a favorite aunt and Margaret Rutherford bore no resemblance to her whatsoever. Rutherford did not wish to play the part either, saying "Murder, you see, is not the sort of thing I could get close to. I never found it amusing. I don't like anything that tends to lower or debase or degrade". It was not until director George Pollack sent her the script for Murder She Said, the first Miss Marple film planned, and convinced her that Miss Marple would be a helpful character, one who took a gamesman-like approach to crime solving. Rutherford was then gung-ho about the part and made Miss Marple completely her own. Her husband and closest companion, Stringer Davis, was pulled in for the ride as well in a part that was created especially for him at Rutherford's insistence. As the timid librarian Jim Stringer, he was the perfect partner for the indomitable Jane.

Rutherford's Miss Marple was a completely transformed character from the St. Mary's Mead citizen that Christie had penned some thirty-five years back. In fact, she did not even live in St. Mary's Mead anymore, her cottage home now being situated in Milchester (filmed in Denham). Here the jaunty heroine lives in contented

peace until a mystery falls at her feet and she takes on the task of solving the crime herself when the local police force doubt her theories - the local police force being Inspector Craddock (admirably played by Australian actor Charles "Bud" Tingwell) and his aide Sergeant Bacon. Craddock was another character written in especially for the film and he proved to be a capital foil in the crime-solving endeavors of Miss Marple. His attitude towards Miss Marple was much like a kindly nephew, loving and protective and yet at times quite aggravated over her interference in police matters and the dangers the old gal was putting herself into.

The sprightly harpsichord strains of Ron Goodwin's Miss Marple theme quickly set the tempo and mood for the films that were to follow, all of them being light-hearted tea and crumpet mysteries. Just as one enjoys curling up with a good mystery before bedtime to carry one off to slumberland, so these films were a relaxing escape from the typical juvenile crime flicks, period dramas, and psychological capers of the times. And, as an added bonus, they

FAMOUS AND FORGOTTEN FILMS

gave us opportunity to nod our heads in blessed slumber during many a scene.

Between 1961 and 1965, Metro-Goldwyn-Mayer made four Miss Marple films starring Margaret Rutherford. Each film in the series was directed by George Pollock and featured scripts written by David Pursall and Jack Seddon. Although none of them bore any resemblance to the books on which they were based, each of them had their redeeming charms and to this day all of the films have their loyal following of fans.

Whatever Miss Christie intended her stories to be, is completely thrown out the window. Margaret Rutherford is the unreputable star of these films. Plump, energetic and commanding, Rutherford created a newly emancipated Miss Marple, a gal brimming with spunk. With jowls jiggling and her tongue jutted firmly in her cheek, Jane would swing her tweed cape about her, square her shoulders and be ready to face any danger that stood in the way of her amateur sleuthing.

Murder She Said (1961)

En route from Paddington station to her home in Milchester, Miss Marple witnesses a murder onboard a passing train. When the authorities investigate and find no clues, Miss Marple is determined to investigate herself. With the help of her good friend Mr. Stringer, they track the body to the Ackenthorpe Estate. Here, she goes undercover as a maid and, in between the housework and the cooking, hunts for clues. The entire family comes for a visit and when the body turns up in the stable, each member, including Miss Marple herself, becomes a suspect.... and one by one start being killed off themselves.

Margaret Rutherford is splendid as the elderly amateur sleuth who is excited to put her knowledge of mystery stories to the test and try crime-detection on a personal level. She proves to be more perceptive than the police and more daring, often jeopardizing herself much to the chagrin of Inspector Craddock, who feels personally responsible for the dear gal's safety.

Our cast of suspects is a colorful lot of crooked family members, each one of them waiting for the blustery old codger, Mr. Ackenthorpe (played with splendid bark by James Robertson Justice) to die so they can inherit his money, his land, and his house. Muriel Pavlow, playing Ackenthorpe's daughter provides the romantic interest in the film with love blossoming between her and the American doctor (Arthur Kennedy) who is looking after the old man. Most engaging of all  the characters however, is cheeky little Alexander (Ronnie Raymond), a playful dodger who tries to hide his mischievous pranks with his overly gentlemanly manner. He and Miss Marple quickly become chums and he provides her with many an inside scoop in the whereabouts of the family skeletons. Thorley Walters, Ron Howard (son of Leslie Howard), Conrad Phillips, Gerald Cross and Joan Hickson round out the cast. Joan Hickson later picked up the Miss Marple mantle herself in a PBS series during the 1980s.

Margaret Rutherford's immense appeal and the delightful mystery plot she was involved with in *Murder She Said* made the film an instant box office success and it was quickly followed by three more Miss Marple mysteries. *Murder She Said* was the only one of the three actually based on one of Agatha Christie's Miss Marple mysteries, "4:50 from Paddington" (known as "What Mrs. McGillicuddy Saw" in Great Britain). A few major alternations from the 1957 novel resulted in a more cohesive and less complicated film. In the novel, Miss Marple is a relatively minor character. In the film however, she takes on the activities of three of the characters from the novel: Mrs. McGillicuddy, who first witnesses the murder, Lucy Eyesbarrow, housekeeper at the Crackenthorpe estate, and herself.

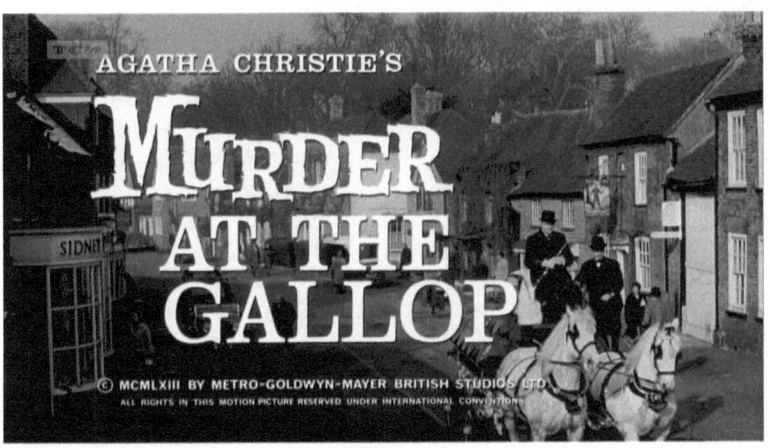

Murder at the Gallop (1963)

George Pollock returned to take the helm in the second Miss Marple movie, *Murder at the Gallop*, this time set at a riding establishment, the Gallop Hotel, where members of the Enderby family are staying. Mr. Enderby, an elderly recluse (played by Finlay Currie), was frightened to death - by a cat - in circumstances that Miss Marple believes was deliberate murder. After Aunt Cora announces those same suspicions to the family members during the reading of the will and is quickly dispatched herself - with a hairpin, by george! - Miss Marple declares "murder most foul" and is off to capture the culprit herself. Once again Inspector Craddock's insistence against her meddling prove useless in stopping the indomitable dame from charging.

Many of the elements used in *Murder She Said* are repeated for this second outing, notably the family inheritance plot line, the eccentric male lead (this time played by the perpetually baffled-faced Robert Morley), the surly stableman, and the multiple murders. Yes, when Miss Marple attempts to solve a case, murder is never a solitary occurrence. Even the finale of Miss Marple receiving a marriage proposal is repeated.

Many of the Enderby family members are not as engaging as the Ackenthorpes however, and this time around most of the entertaining scenes belong solely to Margaret Rutherford, which thankfully there are plenty of. Highlights include Miss Marple and Mr. Stringer collecting donations to help rehabilitate criminals and the duo performing the twist in preparation for the climatic ending. The extremely talented character actress, Flora Robson, has a wonderful part in *Murder at the Gallop* as the frightened companion to Aunt Cora, and Robert Urquhart, Katya Douglas, and James Villiers complete the cast.

Murder at the Gallop was based on the Poirot mystery "After the Funeral". The film had its premiere in a tent at a garden party in rural Cheshire during a fundraiser and once again received good critic reviews after its national premiere. One critic however did not find the film amusing... Agatha Christie called it "incredibly silly" and often argued with Metro-Goldwyn-Mayer over the scripts and characterizations of her stories, but to no avail. The London Times agreed, "The whole thing is happily calculated to convince

foreigners yet again that everything they have been told about the English is absolutely true and only a trifle understated."

Murder Ahoy (1964)

The next Miss Marple film to be released, *Murder Ahoy*, was actually the final one in the series to be filmed, with *Murder Most Foul* being temporarily delayed in its release.

This film has the distinction of being the only one of the four pictures based on an original script, and unfortunately, that was a mistake... the movie suffers badly with long stretches of sleep-inducing sequences. Ron Goodwin's jaunty Marple theme fails to revive one, even in the film's most exciting moments.

One redeeming quality, however, is the change of locale. Filmed at St. Mawes, on the Cornwall coast, *Murder Ahoy* gives one the impression of being on a seaside holiday. Miss Marple enjoys the respite herself and decks herself in full-rigged naval dress complete with brass buttons and tricorn hat. Quite fitting regalia indeed for a trustee of the H.M.S Battledore, a training ship used for

rehabilitating juvenile delinquents. During the annual meeting of the trustees, Mr. Folly-Hardwicke snuffs himself out and drops dead before announcing a most dreadful finding - one of the instructors on board the Battledore is an embezzler!

Miss Marple brings out her trusty Slocum's Chemistry Set for Girls, discovers strychnine in the snuff, shanghais her sweetheart Mr.Stringer, and then boldly sets out to board the Battledore and hoist the culprit on the highest yardarms. She makes an impressive splash and puts every member of the frigate properly ill at ease, before confronting the killer with crossed swords in a climatic finale. "It won't be as easy as you think," she burbles stoutly, "I was ladies' fencing champion in 1931", whereupon she lunges to attack for a swashbuckling finish.

The inimitable character actor Lionel Jeffries plays the eccentric lead, Captain Rhumstone, in this seafaring outing that also features William Mervyn, Francis Matthews, Joan Benham and Gerald Cross.

FAMOUS AND FORGOTTEN FILMS

Murder Most Foul (1965)

In this final installment in the series our doughty heroine finds herself in the blazing spotlights of a stage; a stage where murder and mayhem are being played out. After the former actress Mrs. McGinty is found hanging in her house with roses and money strewn on the floor about her, a young man is promptly arrested as the leading suspect. Miss Marple, serving on the jury during the trial, believes him innocent and decides to prove just that. Clues lead her to the Cosgood Players, a mixed lot of theatrical characters, and to one player in particular, a scheming murderer who kills twice more before Miss Marple drops the final curtain on him.

Ron Moody, best known for his portrayal of Fagin in *Oliver!*, plays the leading supporting character Clifford Cosgood, head of the Cosgood Players and, not unlike Fagin, he is a thoroughly shifty-eyed sort. The marvelous Megs Jenkins has an all too brief appearance as Mrs. Thomas, the dead actress' sister who has taken a bit of a fancy to the dear Mr. Stringer, and Andrew Cruickshank,

Ralph Michael, James Bolam, and Annette Kerr complete our cast of suspects.

Margaret Rutherford gets to recite the splendid piece, "The Shooting of Dan McGrew" during her audition to become one of the Cosgood Players. This was one of Rutherford's favorite pieces and at one time she had to be dissuaded from performing it at a women's prison. "It was a good, bloodcurdling bit, which I thought the poor women would enjoy as they must have been disillusioned by the men in their lives," she said. These are words that prove what a beloved, albeit dotty, character one of the most popular British actresses of all time had.

Murder Most Foul picks up on the pace once again after *Murder Ahoy* dropped the slack, but alas.... it was not enough to draw fans into the theatres in droves and the declining box-office receipts were a sign that the Miss Marple series had reached their end. Such a shame too, for there were so many more good mysteries Margaret Rutherford's Miss Marple could have solved.

FAMOUS AND FORGOTTEN FILMS 203

WALT DISNEY STUDIOS (1963)

Back in the days shortly after the death of Unther Pendragon, King of England, a magic sword appears in London protruding upright from the center of an anvil. It bears an inscription proclaiming that whosoever shall remove the sword from the stone would be crowned the new king of England.

Young Arthur (aka Wart) is an orphan who was raised in Sir Ector's castle. Sir Ector's son, Sir Kay, desires to venture to London to joust in the countrywide competition shortly before Christmas Day. Arthur aspires to be this knight's squire, but while on a hunting trip in the woods with Sir Kay, he falls into the hut of the wizard, Merlin. This kindly old man can see the future as well as the past and, knowing the young lad is fated to draw the sword from the stone, decides to take Arthur under his wing and "give him an education" prior to his crowning as the illustrious King Arthur. With the help of Archimedes the Owl, Merlin teaches Arthur to believe in himself and to use wits over brawn.

The Sword in the Stone is a delightful animated feature from Walt Disney Studios. It features an amnesiac "whiz-bang whizard of whimsy", an engaging young hero and, in place of the usual villain, there is Madam Mim, a rival to Merlin.

The story is based on the Arthurian novels of T.H. White's "The Once and Future King" series. Walt Disney enjoyed the first book - "The Sword in the Stone" - and purchased the film rights to it the same year it was published: 1938. Unfortunately, the project was not picked up until 1949 when some preliminary storyboards were created. Then there was another long hiatus before story artist Bill Peet re-worked it into this film.

While this version of *The Sword in the Stone* is entertaining, it would have benefited greatly from having a stronger villain, some character in the vein of Maleficent ....preferably Morgan le Fay or Vivien, the enchantress who proved to be Merlin's downfall. Madam Mim is an unworthy opponent to both Merlin and Arthur while Sir Ector and his son Sir Kay are more comical than villainous.

Like *101 Dalmation*s released two years earlier, *The Sword in the Stone* implemented Disney's time-saving process of xeroxing the animation cels instead of retracing each cel. Because the Xerox copy machines were only capable of black lines, all of the lines around the figures were inked in black. Some critics feel this technique made the films look inferior to Disney's animated pictures of previous years but, personally, I liked the look.

Richard and Robert Sherman penned some linguistically clever - albeit forgetful - tunes to *The Sword in the Stone*, including the delightful "Higitus Figitus", sung by Merlin.

FAMOUS AND FORGOTTEN FILMS

The Sword in the Stone was released in theaters on Christmas Day in 1963 and proved to be a box-office smash, reaping in nearly $20 million dollars in profit.

WALT DISNEY PICTURES (1964)

In 1963, Hayley Mills, one of the most popular child stars of the decade, set off for Greece to star in Walt Disney's family-friendly adaptation of author Mary Stewart's thrilling novel "The Moon-Spinners".

Mills stars as Nikky Ferris, a young girl who is traveling throughout Europe with her Aunt Frances (Joan Greenwood) to record folk songs for the BBC. They arrive at The Moon-Spinners Inn on the island of Crete where they stumble into a dangerous web of intrigue involving a handsome young Englishman (Peter McEnery) and a desperate jewel smuggler named Stratos (Eli Wallach).

The Moon-Spinners is a delightful mystery-adventure that combines an exciting plot with marvelous Cretian atmosphere. In fact, it is the location filming and exotic setting of *The Moon-Spinners* that truly lends the film its appeal.

"They cannot have lied. The stars cannot lie." - *Stratos*

"Everybody lies when it serves their purpose, even the stars." - *Madame Habib*

Mary Stewart was a prolific British novelist who developed the romantic-mystery genre. Her books, most of which took place in exotic locations throughout Europe, always featured a young heroine who would find romance in the midst of a dangerous situation.

Hayley Mills was quickly growing out of her childhood film roles and this was an ideal production that helped transition her into more mature teen roles. Her character Nikki is headstrong and capable, yet vulnerable enough to need to be rescued by the handsome tourist Mark, portrayed by Peter McEnery. This young English actor was making his American film debut in *The Moon-Spinners* and - while he didn't have the charm of James MacArthur or Kurt Russell - he was perfect for this role. Walt Disney liked this affable young gentleman so much that he starred him in another feature the following year: *The Fighting Prince of Donegal.*

Like most Disney films, *The Moon-Spinners* features an excellent cast of supporting players. Eli Wallach, with his dark glaring eyes, is ideal as Uncle Stratos, a "much lousy man" who would willingly commit murder in his desperation for wealth. The beautiful Grecian actress Irene Papas is given a small but memorable role as Stratos' sister, the owner of The Moon-Spinners Inn.

Joan Greenwood, with her delicious purring voice, is Nikki's aunt. She spends most of her vacation worrying about Nikki's whereabouts, not even knowing that there is a crime being committed right before her eyes. Also in the cast is Greenwood's husband Andre Morrell in a brief part as the captain of The Minotaur, the fabulous yacht owned by Madame Habib, a role that was portrayed by the great silent film star Pola Negri. Walt Disney personally coaxed her out of retirement to make an appearance in the film and she delivers a grand performance.

John Le Mesurier is perfect as the English consulate who lives in a palatial manor overlooking the Mediterranean Sea with his discontented wife, the tipsy "Angel of Eastbourne" portrayed by Sheila Hancock. Paul Stassino (*Thunderball*) is once again playing a villain but most entertaining of all the secondary roles is that of Alexis, delightfully portrayed by Michael Davis. The young Greek lad who aids Nikki and Mark in their escape is actually an American boy! Fancy that.

The Moon-Spinners is unlike other Disney films of the era because it doesn't feature much humor or any musical interludes but it does feature plenty of adventure (the windmill escape and the fantastic ride through the King Minos parade in a hearst are highlights) and a memorable musical score by Ron Grainer. "The Moon-Spinners Song" is especially lovely, evoking the sounds of a traditional Greek folk melody. It was written by Terry Gilkyson and is beautifully performed over the title credits by Gilkyson, Carson and Van Dyke Parks and other members of the folk group The Easy Riders.

COLUMBIA PICTURES (1964)

ROBINSON CRUSOE ON MARS

A lone astronaut pitted against all the odds beyond this earth.

In the not too distant future, a two-manned spacecraft, the Mars Gravity Probe 1, nearly avoids a collision with an asteroid on its route to the red planet. The ship cannot hold altitude after altering its trajectory so the crew eject from the vessel, making a crash landing on Mars.

Only Commander Kit Draper (Paul Mantee) and the ship's monkey Mona survive. His commanding officer Colonel McReady (Adam West) is killed in the collision. Draper leaves the wreckage behind

and, with Mona in tow, proceeds to find shelter on Mars. He assesses his situation, takes stock of his supplies and begins to determine his needs. He finds the atmosphere thin and breathable for only short periods of time and so maintaining a continuous air supply becomes Draper's first priority. Later, he discovers sources of food and water. When alien spaceships come to Mars to recapture an escaped slave (Victor Lundin), Draper is relieved to find another person to converse with and helps the slave "Friday" hide from their watchful eye until they depart.

Robinson Crusoe on Mars is unlike other science-fiction films of the era. While most pictures that were set in outer space pitted a crew of astronauts against a creature or creatures unknown, *Robinson Crusoe on Mars* focused on one man all alone in unfamiliar territory and his struggle to conquer loneliness, a beast more fearsome than any two-headed martian.

Kit Draper strikes us as a modern intelligent human, not giving in to panic and capable of managing in extreme situations. He is a well-trained astronaut. Draper underwent months of vigorous pre-flight training and simulations of what he would encounter on Mars. He is prepared for any and all circumstances... or so he believes. What he is not prepared for is the chasm of loneliness he would feel in his new surroundings. He is grateful for the companionship of his monkey but longs for human conversation. *Robinson Crusoe on Mars* depicts interaction between people as a vital element to human survival, as necessary to man as oxygen or water and it is this facet of the film that makes it more realistic than other sci-fi films of the 1950s.

Paul Mantee considered Draper a difficult character to portray since he had no one to interact with, but he handled the part beautifully. Unlike many films that portray solitary characters, *Robinson Crusoe on Mars* avoided giving audiences a mental voice-over from the main protagonist and instead we discover Draper's thoughts only through his discussions with Mona and his "diary", his recordings of his actions onto video and audio tape.

Victor Lundin had parts in television westerns and other series (primarily portraying Native Americans) before he was given his first starring feature film role as the intergalactic mining slave, Friday. Adam West had very little screen time and what little dialogue he had was uttered in his usual stilted manner but he more than made up for that by his surreal materialization in one truly spine-tingling hallucination sequence. Mona the monkey was portrayed by a talented newcomer named Barney who had to humble himself and endure wearing not only the miniature space-suit costume for the part but a fur-covered diaper as an undergarment.

The premise of Daniel Defoe's beloved 1719 novel "Robinson Crusoe" was transported into the space age by screenwriter Ib

Melchoir who set out to create a realistic portrayal of an astronaut's experience on an unexplored planet. A heady task considering it would be five more years before mankind would even set foot on the moon.

He retained all of the key elements of Defoe's novel - Crusoe's determination to survive, his methods of survival, and his struggle with loneliness - replacing only the cannibals with alien slavers to make the story more plausible. Ironically, it is Melchoir's faithfulness to the book that bogs down the final chapter of the film. Draper's solitary experience of survival and his encounter with the aliens would have made a fascinating picture in itself. The Egyptian-like slave sequence was unnecessary and tiresome.

Like the novel, *Robinson Crusoe on Mars* retains a strong religious subtext running through the film. At just the right moments, Draper's life is spared by the hand of God. Heat, shelter, food, companionship, all become available to him in his hour of need. While Draper may be all alone in the new world, he knows he always has God looking after him, giving him hope.

Crusoe's director, Byron Haskin, had a career stretching back as far as the silent era when he worked as a cinematographer to D.W. Griffith. During the 1930s and 40s, he headed up the visual effects department at Warner Brothers, working on such classics as *The Sea Hawk*, *High Sierra*, and *Dive Bomber*. Haskin had directed some iconic sci-fi films and television series (*War of the Worlds*, *Conquest of Space*, and several episodes of *The Outer Limits*) before taking the helm of Crusoe.

His experience in visual effects is demonstrated in the marvelous long shots where we witness Draper exploring one vast territory of desolate landscape after another with only Albert Whitlock's matte paintings being utilized to create the backdrops of space. This skyline looks majestic and peaceful compared to the steaming hot surface of Mars or its cool polar icecaps. Location footage was shot in Death Valley where the clear skies were used as a natural "blue screen" and enabled the matte paintings to be implemented.

Some of the other special effects in the film seem primitive and will look dated to modern viewers but *Robinson Crusoe on Mars* stands out for these dynamic visualizations of Mars. An entire harsh ecosystem is conveyed through its simple sets. Over fifty years later, it is impressive to see how accurately Mars was depicted in 1964. Wouldn't it be ironic if astronauts of the future land on Mars only to find the same landscape depicted in this film?

Check it out!
If you like this, you'll also like.....

First Men in the Moon (1964)

Against the backdrop of a U.N. mission to the Moon, a doddering nursing home resident (Edward Judd) recounts a previously unknown trip he took to the satellite with his fiancée (Martha Hyer) and the eccentric Professor Cavor (Lionel Jeffries). There, the trio had encountered an insect-like civilization living below the surface, and used all resources at their fingertips to return to Earth. Witty science-fiction adventure, based on H.G. Wells' 1901 novel, features stop-motion creations by Ray Harryhausen.

UNIVERSAL PICTURES (1966)

"The Don Knotts Ghost and Mr. Chicken"

Ephraim Simmons murdered his wife in cold blood and then played the organ before killing himself; the keys are still stained with blood and could never be cleaned off.... even after using Bon-Ami! Or so the rumor goes. It takes a man with spunk, like Luther Heggs, to get to the bottom of the real story.

Heggs (Don Knotts), a timid typesetter for a small-town newspaper, boasts that he can spend the night in the old Simmons

mansion where it is rumored that the ghost of Mr. and Mrs. Simmons still reside. His chance to prove his courage - and impress his sweetheart, Alma Parker (Joan Staley) - comes  when he writes an article on the local "haunted house" which creates such a stir that Luther's boss (Dick Sargeant) challenges "Scoop" to spend a night in the old house and do a follow-up story. During the midnight vigil, the terrified Luther discovers a hidden staircase, the blood-stained organ mysteriously playing by itself, and a portrait painting with shears stabbed right through it.

"It was terrible. It was just terrible. I'll never get over it as long as I live!"

After his story is published, a town picnic is given in honor of Luther's courage, but he soon finds himself embroiled in a libel suit when the Simmons' nephew comes to town and demands that he retract his story or prove to the court that what he saw was not just his imagination playing tricks with him.

Don Knotts had just garnered three Emmys for his role as Barney Fife on *The Andy Griffith Show* from 1960-1966 and, after hearing that Griffith intended on ending the series after the fifth season, began to embark on a film career. While Knotts had a few minor roles in feature films *(It's a Mad, Mad, Mad, Mad World; Move Over, Darling)* it was not until 1964 that he received star billing in Warner Brother's *The Incredible Mr. Limpet*. This picture was received poorly at the box-office, however, Lew Wasserman screened the film over at Universal and decided that had *Mr. Limpet* been made by a studio with experience in

FAMOUS AND FORGOTTEN FILMS

family pictures it would have met with great success. Knotts was then offered a five-picture contract and given free rein to screenwriters and key personnel. Atta boy, Don Knotts!

Screen-writers Everett Greenbaum and Jim Fritzell teamed up with Andy Griffith to create a spine-tickling film that spotlighted Knott's unique comedic flair and combined all of the homespun humor of *The Andy Griffith Show*. A plethora of familiar character actors portrayed the citizens of the fictional small town of Rachel, Kansas, including a motherload of Mayberry-ites such as Hal Smith (Otis) as the town drunk , Hope Summers (Clara), Ellen Corby (in an amusing sequence as Hegg's former schoolteacher) and Burt Mustin (Jud).

The Ghost and Mr. Chicken is packed with humorous one-liners but it is not the script that makes the film the memorable comedy classic that it is - it is these character actors and the brilliant facial expressions they display with every line. Jesslyn Fax stands out as Hegg's adorable landlady and Reta Shaw gives a beefy performance as the leader of the ladies' Psychic Occult Society ("Taro, Karo, Salome!").

"I was only two blocks away that awful night, at my sister Clara's. We were sort of... listening.. to the organ, you know... the midnight bells were ringing... I turned to Clara and said, 'Clara, the organ music sounds straaange tonight!'.....

However, Don Knotts needed no support when it came to getting an audience to laugh. His nervous speech at the town picnic is a tour-de-force of comedic timing and remains one of the highlights of the film. Another memorable scene takes place at the diner - Luther leaves his seat beside Alma for a moment and a truck driver takes it, leaving Luther to slurp his soup from a standing position. Only Knotts can portray such a lovable small-town boob (he even drives an Edsel!).

Production on *The Ghost and Mr. Chicken* began in July 1965 and wrapped up within seventeen days, thanks to a swift television crew behind the cameras. Since the picture had a low budget most of it was filmed on the Universal backlot. The famous Simmons mansion was a long-standing structure originally built in the 1940s and used for many Universal classics including *Harvey* (1950). Keep an eye out for the Munster mansion next door at 1313 Mockingbird Lane.

"Calm? Do 'murder' and 'calm' go together? Calm and murder?!"

FAMOUS AND FORGOTTEN FILMS

"THE GHOST AND MR. CHICKEN" (I-A)

While most of the cast and crew knew what an entertaining film they were making, they did not realize just how popular it would become. Universal decided to release *The Ghost and Mr. Chicken* as a double-feature with *Munsters, Go Home!* to test the waters, not certain whether audiences wanted to watch two hours worth of Knottisms. Within one week of its release *The Ghost* raked in $1,500,000, nearly double its initial cost and in cities across America the film was extended for weeks to packed houses.

A sprightly ghost theme by Vic Mizzy (based on "Mr. Ghost Goes to Town") and a marvelous "haunted" organ anthem permeate this Midwestern comedy gem filled with frightfully funny moments, a chilling atmosphere, stellar character actors, and one of Don Knotts' greatest nerve-rattled performances, making it appealing for all ages and the perfect film for a Halloween night.

AUDREY HEPBURN AND PETER O'TOOLE

WILLIAM WYLER'S

HOW TO STEAL A MILLION

20th CENTURY-FOX (1966)

HOW TO STEAL a MILLION

Audrey Hepburn loved Paris and audiences adored seeing her in Paris on film. She portrayed a young woman who journeyed to Paris to study cooking in *Sabrina* (1954), a shy bookshop clerk who longs to see the city in *Funny Face* (1957), and the daughter of a French private detective in *Love in the Afternoon* (1957). In the 1960s she was in love with William Holden in *Paris When it Sizzles* (1963) and that same year chased by four enemies throughout the city in the Hitchcockian suspense classic *Charade*. In 1966, Hepburn returned to Paris for one final outing, this time in the delightful caper *How to Steal a Million*, directed by William Wyler.

Wyler had a flair for sophisticated comedy and *How to Steal a Million* is reminiscent of the snappy comedies of the 1930s with its elegant setting and clever dialogue. Hepburn stars as Nicole Bonnet, the daughter of the world famous art collector Charles Bonnet (Hugh Griffith). Occasionally Monsieur Bonnet auctions some of his beloved paintings for "vast sums of money" and they pass into the hands of other avid

collectors. What the buying public does not realize is that the paintings auctioned from the Bonnet collection are fakes - meticulously created by "Papa" Bonnet himself. Nicole wishes he would stop forging paintings and loaning their personal sculptures to museums, fearing they will one day be caught.... especially since modern methods of examination could determine "the age of the stone, where it was quarried, when it was cut... and probably the name and address of the man who did it!".

"Papa, the Cellini Venus is a fake!"

"That's a word we don't use in this house."

Her fears are realized when their Cellini Venus sculpture, which Bonnet generously loaned to the Kléber-Lafayette Museum of Art, is scheduled to undergo a vigorous chemical examination as a preliminary insurance requirement. Rather than arousing suspicion by recalling the sculpture from the museum, Nicole turns to Simon Dermott (Peter O'Toole), a professional jewel thief, to steal the Cellini Venus back. He and Nicole sneak into the museum at night and using only a magnet, a boomerang, and his wits, attempt to steal a million-dollar art treasure.

"Why must it be this particular work of art?"

"Why, you don't think I'd steal something that doesn't belong to me, do you?"

How to Steal a Million was one of my grandmother's favorite films. Oma Rozi spent happy years in Paris and loved the city dearly. She also loved the lifestyle of the Bonnets, especially Papa's secret attic

room. So this film is particularly dear to me. It boasts a marvelous cast, a witty script, a memorable score by John Williams (credited as "Johnny Williams"), and chic Givenchy costumes (Hepburn dazzled in no less than eight different outfits) but what makes the film a true delight is its setting - Paris.

The movie avoids the cobbled streets and earthy cafe life of Paris that is often portrayed in Hollywood films and instead shows us elegant Paree - a world of high fashion, fancy sports cars, museums, private jets, and auction houses - the setting one likes to associate with the life of an art collector. The film was shot in and around the city and gives us glimpses of the famous Ritz hotel, the Musée Carnavalet, the Élysées Palace along the Champs-Élysées, Maxim's, the Place Vendome, and the Rond-point des Champs-Élysées. The Bonnet's beautiful maison was located on the Rue Parmentier at Carrefour Bineau in Neuilly-sur-Seine, France, but alas... it has since been torn down.

A number of fine French actors add to the film's authentic Parisian flavor; Charles Boyer has a small and insignificant part as DeSolny, the owner of a rival auction house, and the popular comedian Moustache is featured as one of the museum's guards who likes to take a nip when he can. Fernand Gravey, Marcel Dalio, Jacques Marin, and Roger Treville also have parts while American actor Eli Wallach has the best supporting role, that of Mr. Leland, a fanatic art collector wanting to marry Nicole just to get his hands on her Cellini Venus sculpture.

Harry Kurnitz, a prolific screenwriter of the 1930s-1960s, penned the screenplay which was based on a short story "Venus Rising" from "Practice to Deceive" written by George Bradshaw in 1962. Unlike most capers of the 1960s, *How to Steal a Million* does not focus solely on the planning and execution of the heist, instead Kurnitz lets a series of amusing situations unfold, all of which lead to the final heist and, of course, Bonnet and Dermott falling in love. L'Amour dans Paris…what could be a more fitting ending?

PARAMOUNT BRITISH PICTURES (1967)

Half a Sixpence

"But when I'm with you, one and one make two...."

Prior to leaving for London for his apprenticeship at a tailor shop, Arthur gives his childhood sweetheart Ann a token of his eternal love - a sixpence cut in half. "And though that half a sixpence can only mean half a romance, remember that half a romance is better than none. But when I'm with you, one and one make two, and likewise, two half sixpence joined together make one."

It is a sweet sign of a little boy's affection for his girl and throughout their adolescence they correspond with each other daily via letters. One day, Ann (Julia Foster) comes up to London to begin her new job in the big city and they arrange to meet in the park, seeing each other for the first time in years. They are two of a kind and are obviously meant for each other, but an unexpected inheritance from Arthur's grandfather leaves the lad suddenly rich and this enormous windfall changes his character making him look for happiness outside of his own backyard. Arthur begins to put on airs

and takes a fancy to the fetching socialite Miss Helen (Penelope Horner), disowning the company of not only his mates at work but Ann as well.

Half a Sixpence was based on the 1905 novel "Kipps: The Story of a Simple Soul" by science-fiction author H.G. Wells. It was first brought to the screen in 1941 as *Kipps* starring Michael Redgrave and Diana Wynyard. This was a beautiful adaptation but purely dramatic, with no musical numbers. It was not until 1963 that David Heneker wrote 15 songs for the musical adaptation which premiered in London's West End theatre district.

Tommy Steele, a British singing sensation, starred in this stage production. He was a glove-fit for the role of Arthur Kipps. When the stage show was brought to film in 1967, Steele was already establishing a screen-presence for himself through films such as *Tommy the Toreador*, *The Dream Maker*, and *The Happiest Millionaire*. Steele had a joie de vivre that made him a delight to watch on stage and onscreen. His toothy grin would light up any scene that he was in. In *Half a Sixpence*, he practically carries the entire film on his own bony shoulders. While the rest of the cast is pleasant enough to watch, they are all really supporting roles to Kipps.

Julia Foster (Alfie) dyed her hair from blonde to brown to play Ann and is charming as Kipps sweetheart. Also in the cast is Pamela Brown, a favorite of director Michael Powell; Cyril Ritchard, a legendary ham; Penelope Horner, always looking lovely in soft-focus; James Villiers, and Jean Anderson.

FAMOUS AND FORGOTTEN FILMS

Half a Sixpence was aimed toward a more youthful audience and includes a few typical swingin' 60s show scenes and zany moments. Heneker's tunes are easy on the ears with "Half a Sixpence" and "If the Rains Gonna Fall" being the most memorable of all the songs.

What stands out most in the film is the beautiful cinematography by Geoffrey Unsworth. This man was responsible for the gorgeous filming of British classics such as *Scott of the Antartic*, *Trio*, *Turn the Key Softly*, and *A Night to Remember*. Most of Half of Sixpence takes place in the autumn and Unsworth brought out the beauty of the golden hues of England during that time of year.

Director George Sidney, an excellent director from the golden age of MGM musicals *(The Harvey Girls, Annie Get Your Gun, Show Boat, Kiss Me Kate)* did great work with *Half a Sixpence*. The only disappointing aspect of the film is its length. Some scenes - mainly the musical numbers - are unnecessary or drawn-out excessively. This seems to have been a fad with musicals in the late 1960s - *Hello, Dolly!*, *Doctor Dolittle*, and *Goodbye, Mr. Chips* are all over two hours in runtime. Overall, *Half a Sixpence* is not half that bad and if the rains gonna fall then it's a great film to sit back and enjoy.

NUGGET REVIEWS

"There's gold in them thar films!"

THAT CERTAIN AGE (1938) *14k*

A young girl falls in love with a visiting reporter at her family estate. He tries his best to snap her out of her puppy love. Deanna Durbin, Jackie Cooper, Melvyn Douglas, John Halliday, Irene Rich, Nancy Carroll. Universal Pictures. Directed by Edward Ludwig.

Ah yes, the puppy love age. In this case, who could blame Alice for falling in love with the dashing Vincent (Melvyn Douglas)? *Sigh*. The film starts off rather slow but picks up in pace midway through with Durbin singing the lovely tune "My Own". Cooper was just seventeen when this film was made and he plays again with his co-star from *The Champ* (1932), Irene Rich. *That Certain Age* marks the final film appearance of silent actress Nancy Carroll who was rumored to have received more fan mail than any other actress in Hollywood during the 1930s..

THE QUIET MAN (1952) *24k*

A former boxer comes to Ireland to purchase his mother's cottage and make a new life for himself, but first he must square himself with his wife, who believes him to be a coward for not putting up a fight for her dowry. John Wayne, Maureen O'Hara, Barry Fitzgerald, Victor MacLaglen, Mildred Natwick. Republi Pictures. Directed by John Ford.

This is one of those beautiful films where everything falls into place perfectly...the cast, the script, the music, the cinematography, the locations. It just couldn't be any better than it is. It ranks as one of John Ford's greatest films (if not his best) and certainly one of the finest pictures to ever come out of Republic Pictures. You'll be spouting *Quiet Man*-isms forever after viewing this film. "And who taught you to be playing patty fingers in the Holy water?".

FATHER GOOSE (1964) *18k*

A boozie boat bum gets recruited by the British Navy to help with plane-spotting on a secluded Pacific island. While there he - reluctantly - rescues a group of schoolgirls along with their attractive teacher. Cary Grant, Leslie Caron, Trevor Howard, a group of little girls. Universal. Directed by Ralph Nelson.

This is one entertaining film! No matter how many times you see it, it will always put a smile on your face. Cary Grant is excellent as "Mother Goose", the rum-hunting recluse who tries his best to stay out of the war, as is Leslie Caron and Trevor Howard. A fun and adventurous comedy.

20TH CENTURY-FOX (1969)

The Prime of Miss Jean Brodie

"I am in the business of putting old heads on young shoulders and all of my girls are the créme de la créme."

Miss Jean Brodie (Maggie Smith) has dedicated her life, the prime of her life, to her gairls, a class of impressionable students at Marcia Blain's School for Girls in Edinburgh. Forsooth, there are four girls in particular that she hand-picked to nurture, mold, and carry forth into the world the ideologies, etiquette, and culture of the Brodie manifesto:

Mary MacGregor (Jane Carr), a stuttering simple-minded child who worships her; Monica (Shirley Steadman) a literary who Miss Brodie predicts will one day become an actress; Jenny (Diane Greyson), a young beauty whom Miss Brodie feels a spiritual bond with, and whom she believes is destined to become a great lover; and Sandy (Pamela Franklin). "What shall I say about Sandy?".... "Sandy is dependable," Sandy replies.

Indeed, all of Miss Brodie's girls are dependable....and loyal to her. Or so Jean believes, until one day she is informed of her dismissal by the school board and discovers that it was one of her set who "betrayed" her with accusations that she was corrupting the minds of her pupils with fascist politics.

"You are dangerous and unwholesome, and children should not be exposed to you!"

"The Prime of Miss Jean Brodie", Muriel Spark's most celebrated work, was penned in 1961 and has since become known as one of the great contemporary works of fiction. It is a slim, sparse, and brittle novella, written with exactness and compassionate wit. Her story of the charismatic schoolteacher and the effect she has on her pupils was inspired by Miss Kay, a teacher at the Edinburgh School of Girls that Spark attended in her youth. "What filled our minds with wonder and made Miss Kay so memorable was the personal drama and poetry within which everything in her classroom happened."

Jay Presson Allen expanded upon the book when writing the script to *The Prime of Miss Jean Brodie*, which was based upon her own stage play (Vanessa Redgrave starred in the original 1966 London production). Whereas the film follows a natural progression of time, Mrs. Spark moves back and forth in her narrative. We follow six girls of Miss Brodie's "set" throughout their school years, but we also see their middle age and how they looked back with amusement on a Miss Brodie who was beyond her prime. It is only Sandy, the "clever" one, now Sister Helena, a nun, who has compassion for the woman she ultimately betrays, understanding her weaknesses.

"Give me a girl at an impressionable age and she is mine for life"

Miss Brodie believes that deep in all of us is the potential for greatness, or the potential to inspire greatness. As a teacher - first, last, and always - she fiercely defends the freedom she has, and the power she wields, in her ability to inspire her students to think beyond conventional standards. She nurtures their independent spirit ("phrases like the 'team spirit' are always employed to cut across individualism") and admirably imparts to them a passionate love for history, music, literature, and beauty in nature. While other students eat together in the common cafeteria, Miss Brodie and her girls have picnics under the shady boughs of the chestnut tree outdoors.

Brodie's antithesis is the prim and proper headmistress Miss MacKay, played by the brilliant Celia Johnson. MacKay belongs to a respectable old set, an admirer of Stanley Baldwin and his belief in Safety First. But as Miss Brodie informs her girls, "Safety does not come first. Goodness, Truth, and Beauty come first."

Miss MacKay is jealous of the dedication and admiration Jean inspires in her pupils. Like the other girls, Sandy admires Miss Brodie too, but she questions her teachings and comes, in time, to see Miss Brodie's deep-rooted love of art and beauty warp into a misguided and sordid manipulation of her girls. Miss Brodie's own sense of purity denies her from indulging in any physical display of passion for the art teacher Mr. Lloyd (Robert Stephens), her true love, or for Mr. Lowther (Gordon Jackson), the singing master, who wishes to marry her. However, she delights in the idea of one of her set becoming Lloyd's mistress.

Her admiration for men and women who fight for what they believe in causes her to praise figures such as Benito Mussolini and

Franco as conquerors, men who will go down in history as dedicated warriors; and her rousing speeches in praise of these Fascisti causes Mary MacGregor to head into the fray of battle in Spain, dying a fool's death. Sandy alone cares enough to react and, cruel in her awakened moral conscience, she exacts a revenge that will doom her teacher to a bitter and solitary spinsterhood.

The Prime of Miss Jean Brodie was a critical and box office success upon its release in 1969. Its opening theme song "Jean" (written by Rod McKuen and performed by Oliver) went on to top the billboard charts.

Maggie Smith is a triumph in her Oscar-winning portrayal of the captivating teacher and Pamela Franklin gives a particularly strong performance, but it is director Ronald Neame - an artist who was basking in his prime at the time - who deserves credit for making *The Prime of Miss Jean Brodie* such a brilliant film, both visually and dramatically.

Through this picture, he accomplished what almost all filmmakers hope to accomplish when adapting a book to film - to create a picture that not only does justice to its origin but improves upon it. And as Miss Brodie would probably agree - one should always strive for perfection in any art form.

Check it out!
If you like this, you'll also like......

TO SIR, WITH LOVE (1967)

Sidney Poitier stars as a first-year teacher at a rundown East End London secondary school who bucks the traditional educational system, allowing his unruly students to learn through experience and acquire a sense of responsibility. Surprise box-office hit version of E. R. Braithwaite's 1959 autobiographical novel co-stars Judy Geeson, Christian Roberts, Suzy Kendall, and Lulu.

LES FILMS DU CARROSSE (1971)

LES DEUX ANGLAISES ET LE CONTINENT

While recovering at home from a leg injury, Claude (Jean-Pierre Léaud) meets Anne Brown (Kika Markham), the daughter of his mother's old friend, who has come to France to study art. She invites Claude to spend the summer with her sister Muriel (Stacey Tendeter) and her mother at their seaside cottage in Wales, an invitation that he accepts. Once there, Anne conspires to play matchmaker between Claude and Muriel and, over the course of the summer, succeeds. Claude wishes to marry Muriel but she feels that this is only a passing infatuation and declines his offer but later changes her mind. Their parents come to the decision that it is best if they were to separate for a year and then, if they still feel the desire to marry, they may do so. But once back in Paris, Claude has affairs with other women and does indeed realize that his love for

Muriel was temporary. Anne, who is once again in Paris studying art, begins to see Claude more often and the two embark on an affair themselves.

Les Deux Anglaises et Le Continent aka *Two English Girls* was based on the 1956 novel of the same name by Henri-Pierre Roché who also wrote "Jules et Jim". That novel told the story of a young woman who was in love with two men. "Les Deux Anglaises" inverts this premise. The book and the film center on Claude's indecision between his feelings for both sisters whom he met while yet a teenager. It is set during the early 1900s and spans nearly twenty years of Claude's life. It is a sad story but one which the audience can easily relate to. Claude obviously enjoyed his summer with both sisters and, as he got older, found it difficult to love one without the possibility of exploring his feelings for the other sister as well. Once having done so, he was all the more confused about whom he really loved the most.

It is harder for the audience to sympathize with Muriel. She feels as though she is unworthy of Claude even though she knows him to be untrue to her, and so she continues to spurn him...which only serves to drive him away.

FAMOUS AND FORGOTTEN FILMS

The film is filled with many beautiful images symbolic of what the characters are feeling, but it is also very crude, very frank, and quite erotic. Director Francois Truffaut (who also directed *Jules et Jim*) acknowledged that "the film was so romantic, possibly even melodramatic, that it had to be balanced by some very physical scenes." This did not go over well with audiences. In France, the reception to the film was so bad that Truffaut pulled it from the theatres and re-edited it. Years later, he succeeded in adding back twenty minutes that he had originally cut.

"Rather than a film about physical love, I have tried to make a physical film about love." - *Truffaut*

The harsh reception that the picture received disappointed Truffaut who considered it to be his best film up to that time. It has only been in recent decades that *Les Deux Anglaises et Le Continent* has been acknowledged to be the fine film that it is.

Les Deux Anglaises is not a happy picture and it is devoid of humor, but it is beautiful, both in its cinematography (by Nestor Almendros) and in its soulful expression of despair. The film plays out like a novel. It is filled with numerous vignettes that resemble short rich chapters that you want to re-read again and again. Almendros avoids close-ups and, instead, stunning long shots of the Welsh landscape are mixed with medium shots and various techniques from Truffaut's bag of tricks which include superimpositions, lightning-fast cuts, fade-ins and the iris effect (reminiscent of *The Music Man*).

"Between them was a dead girl whom they would not name. Only a child would restore the trio that they once were."

Kika Markham is excellent as level-headed Anne, as is Stacey Tendeter as Muriel, who appears to be more sensible than she acts. However, Jean-Pierre Léaud makes a rather childlike main character. His thin frame emphasizes his boyish features. Perhaps this was what Truffaut intended, but a stronger leading man would have made the film even more compelling. Claude, who puts on the airs of being a mature adult, seems to be only a boy who cannot make up his mind to what - or whom - he desires.

Throughout the film, there is the voice of the narrator who acts as an omniscient presence to relate to us the feelings of the characters, primarily Claude. Without the authoritative voice of this narration (the voice of Truffaut himself), the film may have suffered from relying upon only Léaud's presence.

While the characters in the novel were based on Henri-Pierre Roché's own feelings, Truffaut felt that the novel also reflected the situation that the Bronte sisters were in, with both of them longing for the love of their half-brother Branwell. Throughout the film, Claude and Muriel relate to going back to their "brother-sister" relationship, realizing they could never be lovers when they feel such a close sibling-like bond to each other.

Truffaut also suffused the film with a sadness which he was experiencing at the time. Shortly before filming began, Truffaut had been treated for severe depression. Like Claude, he too was in love with two sisters - the actresses Catherine Deneuve and Françoise Dorléac - one of whom had died only three years before he began work on the film.

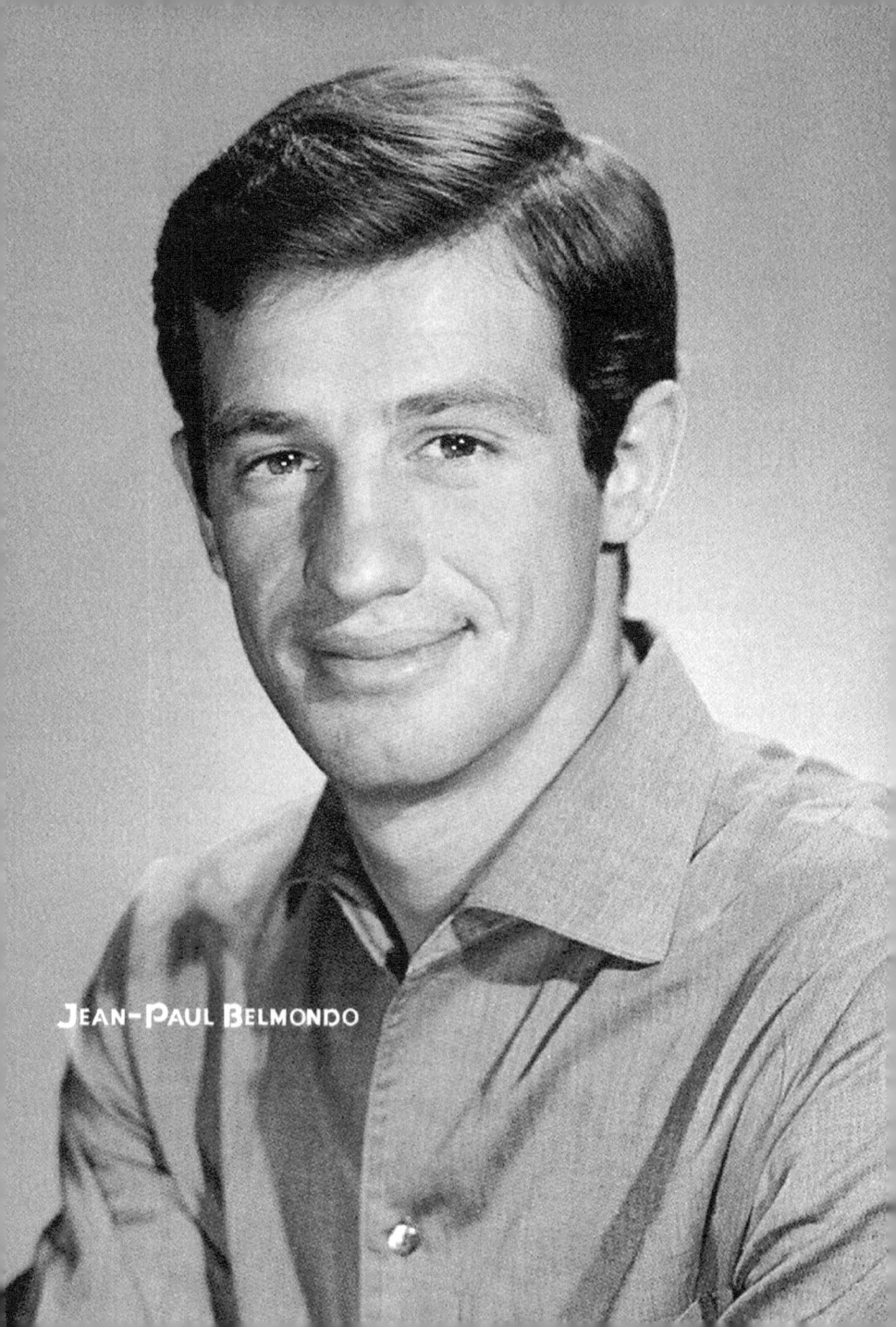

EMI FILMS (1971)

Mr. FORBUSH and the PENGUINS

Richard Forbush is a rich young philanderer. He likes to woo girls and wear smart-looking clothes to college. His professor considers him to be one of the most academically brilliant students in his class with "the potential to be an outstanding biologist," but Forbush has little interest in biology, only mating.

One day, he meets Tara (Hayley Mills), the new waitress at his local pub and, smitten with her, attempts to impress her with tales of how he will go "down the Amazon" and be one of the last men to undertake a great scientific adventure. When his professor offers him the opportunity to live the great adventure by spending six months in Antarctica tracking the population and habits of a penguin colony, he turns it down.... until a casual remark made by Tara changes his mind.

> *"That's all you are. Wind. Empty wind."*

He is aghast that Tara does not succumb to his charms and is downright offended when she calls him "empty wind". He decides to accept the position after all but begins to regret it soon after.

> *"It's a grim prospect, all that ice. I don't know how I am going to get back in one piece. I feel rather like poor Captain Oates. Remember what he said when he walked into the blizzard to die, 'I'm just going outside and may be some time'"*

Within a few weeks, Forbush is dropped off at Shackleton's Hut at Cape Royds with a two-way radio being his only link to the outside world. He is told not to interfere with nature but he grows attached to the penguins he is studying and their plight to survive. After months of watching skuas steal the penguins' eggs, he attempts to destroy them by building a catapult to hurl rocks at them. All is in vain and Forbush comes home realizing that every living creature depends in some way upon every other.

Mr. Forbush and the Penguins, also released as *Cry of the Penguins*, is not your typical arctic adventure film. Instead of the man-battling-the-elements plot line, this film focuses on how six months spent alone with penguins can change a man. It does indeed transform Mr. Forbush dramatically.

John Hurt gives a wonderful sensitive portrayal of the young playboy turned penguin fancier. It is hard to imagine that the man throwing rocks at the invading skuas at the end of the film is the same Mr. Forbush who showed little to no interest in arctic birds at the beginning of the picture. Hurt has such a marvelously silky voice that it is a pleasure to hear him narrate the penguin sequences. Hayley Mills also gives a good performance in what is strangely listed on the credits as a guest appearance. Also in the cast is Tony Britton as Forbush's professor, Dudley Sutton, Thorley Walters, and Judy Campbell.

FAMOUS AND FORGOTTEN FILMS

The production for *Mr. Forbush and the Penguins* was rather rocky. Alfred Viola, a commercial director, was making his directorial debut when he signed on for the production but mid-way through was dismissed by producer Roy Boulting, who took over directing himself. Boulting also put his wife Hayley Mills in the role of Tara, in place of Susan Fleetwood, whom Hurt preferred. Swedish director Arne Sucksdorff flew to the Arctic for location filming and captured some beautiful footage of the penguins in their natural habitat while John Addison (Tom Jones) created a compelling score for the film.

Unfortunately, after all that effort (and a nearly £600,000 investment), *Mr. Forbush and the Penguins* tanked at the box office. The publicity department mistakenly tried to publicize the movie as a comedy, plastering the posters with corny taglines like "It's not often that 740,000 penguins can help a love affair!" and "the zaniest bunch of birds on the South Pole!".

If one is looking for comedy, then this film would fall short. In fact, the first 15 minutes are rather a drag. But after the professor hands Forbush his opportunity to become an explorer of old, the film becomes an absorbing blend of documentary and drama. A look into the life of one man and over half-a-million tuxedo-clad arctic birds.... quite a novel idea for a film. And speaking of novels, if you want to enjoy this story in print, read Graham Billing's original 1965 novel "Forbush and the Penguins".

COLUMBIA PICTURES (1974)

The Golden Voyage of Sinbad

Exotic adventure, thrills and romance were all to be had in *The Golden Voyage of Sinbad*, the second of three Sinbad movies that special-effects animator Ray Harryhausen helped to create during the 1950s-1970s. The first film - *The 7th Voyage of Sinbad* (1958) - was a storybook Arabian Nights fantasy that combined an exciting tale of adventure with amazing stop-motion animated creatures, a powerful Bernard Herrmann score, and beautiful location scenery. It was extremely popular with children and adults alike during its initial release, but its creators, Harryhausen and producer Charles Schneer, had several other projects in the stewpot and did not concentrate on developing another Sinbad film to follow up on its success until the early 1970s.

This film, aptly titled *The Golden Voyage of Sinbad*, found the turbaned sailor (John Philip Law) on a quest for the missing pieces of an ancient golden tablet that points the way to an island which contains a mythical fountain granting eternal wealth and power to the man who bathes in its waters. Over land and sea Sinbad journeyed with the evil magician Koura (Tom Baker) ever on his tail. Koura desperately sought the restoring power of the fountain because his life force was draining out of him with every incantation he chanted.

This story plot provided Ray Harryhausen with ample opportunities to pit various creatures against our hero and the film featured some of Harryhausen's best Dynamation work including the bat-like Homonicus, a messenger to Koura; the wooden figurehead which comes to life; the terrifying centaur; and the griffin, defender of the magic fountain. Also, who could possibly forget the six-armed statue of Kali? Despite being slow on its feet, it was nimble with its swordplay.

Aside from creating the stop-motion sequences of mythical creatures and other characters, Harryhausen helped flesh out the stories to almost all of the films he worked on. He also created extremely detailed storyboards allowing the directors to simply follow each block like a comic book.

The Golden Voyage of Sinbad was three years in the making with Harryhausen spending one year strictly at work filming the creatures. Critical reception was generally negative upon its release but that did not deter its creators from making a third Sinbad film several years later - *Sinbad and the Eye of the Tiger* (1977).

Screenwriter Brian Clemens (of *The Avengers* fame) penned a marvelous script for *The Golden Voyage of Sinbad* filled with nonstop action. Combined with the talented cast, a sweeping Miklos Rozsa score, and Harryhausen's "magic", it has now gained the rightful reputation of being the best of the Sinbad series.

Of the three actors who portrayed Sinbad in each of the Harryhausen pictures, John Philip Law, the star of *The Golden*

Voyage of Sinbad, was certainly the most convincing, capturing the adventurous spirit and the inspiring leadership of the fabled sailor. With Law portraying Sinbad, it is easy to see why his sailors followed him to the four corners of the world.

Tom Baker is also excellent as Koura, the master of the black arts, with his intense eyes and imposing presence. Christopher Lee was originally slated to play this part, but through a stroke of good fortune Baker was cast. This film would be instrumental in Baker obtaining the role of the fourth doctor in the television series, *Doctor Who*.

Also cast in the film was Caroline Munro as the buxom slave girl Marinda, Douglas Wilmer as the mysterious gold-masked vizier, and Kurt Christian as Sinbad's friend Haroun, included for comic relief.

WALT DISNEY STUDIOS (1974)

The ISLAND at the TOP of the WORLD

"Where the whales go to die. All those great creatures from every sea, lying there, from the beginning of time."

Island at the Top of the World, an adventure film from Walt Disney Studios, has fallen into oblivion just like the burial grounds of the whales that the heroes of the picture are searching for.

The arctic graveyard turns out to be quite an amazing sight...and so does the film, which combines a fun and thrilling plot with a fantastic visual theme. It takes place at the turn of the century and tells the story of an English aristocrat who employs the aid of a French airship captain and an American scientist to go to the Arctic to find his son, who went missing during an expedition to find the legendary whale burial grounds. In their quest for him, they discover a hidden island of Vikings untouched by civilization.

FAMOUS AND FORGOTTEN FILMS

Walt Disney Studios had made some stellar adventure films in the 1950s and 1960s such as *20,000 Leagues Under the Sea*, *Swiss Family Robinson*, and *In Search of the Castaways*. However, after Disney's death in 1966, the studio was captained by a committee and the production values of their films declined drastically.

Island at the Top of the World was the studio's attempt to recapture the glory days of Disney's live-action films and create an entertaining adventure picture for children and adults alike. As far as that goal was concerned, they accomplished it...but it took a few decades before the film found its audience. *Island at the Top of the World* was a dismal failure during its initial theatrical release.

The reason behind this? The timing just wasn't right. Critics and audiences during the early 1970s wanted something more than an old-fashioned steam-punk style adventure film. Also, the actors are not as engaging as they could have been, even though they handle their parts very well and, watching the film, you get a feeling that

it was hurriedly assembled. Had Walt Disney been alive during its production the cast would have been top-notch, and the special effects made better. In truth, the film was six years in production, so time was not an issue. As far back as 1968 the studio was planning storyboard drawings to create this adaptation of Ian Cameron's 1961 book "The Lost Ones".

The primary disappointment was the use of painted mattes throughout the film. In spite of being excellently painted by Peter Ellenshaw and Alan Maley, they hinder the realism of the picture during the action sequences. A less heavy reliance on the blue-screen, and the use of miniatures for the villages and volcanoes would have been better. These are the only major flaws in the film, however. The sequences of the airship "Hyperion" sailing through the foggy skies were extremely well filmed for its time and Maurice Jarre (*Lawrence of Arabia*) composed a memorable score for *Island at the Top of the World*, using ancient Nordic instruments to add to the film's authenticity.

Donald Sinden, David Hartman, and Jacques Marin portray the principal characters with Mako playing a large supporting role as

their Eskimo guide. David Gwillim and Agneta Eckemyr come in mid-way through the film to provide some youthful love interest as well. The characters travel high above icebergs, journey into a volcano, fight off killer whales, and are chased throughout the island by a mad and powerful Norseman known as the Godi, before they are able to escape back to Paris.

If you are looking for an entertaining and action-packed film to watch on a Saturday evening, then don't steer away from *Island at the Top of the World*. It packs in more than its fair share of thrills and leaves you with the urge to set off on your own reckless journey into the skies with an airship. Great fun!

Check it out!
If you like this, you'll also like.....

IN SEARCH OF THE CASTAWAYS (1962)

Mary Grant (Hayley Mills) and her younger brother attempt to convince Lord Glenarvan (Wilfrid Hyde White) that their father Captain Grant is still alive and lost somewhere in the South Pacific. They then set sail on an adventure that takes them to Australian isles in their quest to find him. Maurice Chevalier and George Sanders co-star.

Julie Andrews Omar Sharif

The Tamarind Seed

LORIMAR FILMS (1974)

The Tamarind Seed

Judith Farrow (Julie Andrews) is still grieving over the breakup of a rather lurid liaison with her married paramour Group Captain Richard Patterson (David Baron). She is vacationing in Barbados, attempting to clear her muddled mind and heal her broken heart, when she meets the suave Colonel Feodor Sverdlov (Omar Shariff), a Soviet military attaché who is also vacationing for a respite. Feodor works in the Paris embassy circle and happens to know Captain Patterson. Coincidentally, he is also acquainted with Sam Neilson of the British Home Office, for whom Judith works as a personal assistant.

Back in London, British intelligence officer Jack Loder (Anthony Quayle) and Home Secretary Fergus Stephenson (Daniel O'Herlihy) are curious as to why Feodor is in Barbados and decide to keep surveillance on him and his supposedly coincidental encounter with Judith. Loder believes Feodor is conspiring to win Judith over "to the other side" so that the Russians could use her as an inside agent.

Judith thought she met a kind and understanding friend on her holiday but when Loder approaches her with his suspicions of Feodor's motives for meeting her, she begins to wonder if she is indeed being used as a pawn in a political chess game between the East and the West.

The Tamarind Seed is an engrossing romantic espionage drama from director Blake Edwards. It is a long picture (125-minutes) and the pace is slow, yet the story is riveting and the film never becomes tiresome. This is due to the fine performances of all the principal players and Edwards' compelling script, which was based on Evelyn Anthony's 1971 bestselling novel.

Julie Andrews, who was married to Edwards at the time, delivers an excellent performance as the bewildered Ms. Farrow. Andrews portrays Judith as a woman of intelligence and strength, lost and confused though she may be. Judith follows her heart, in spite of being warned against doing so. "He's going to recruit you, isn't he?" Loder tells her. "You're wrong. He'll never do anything like that. I know him." "Do you? I doubt that, Mrs. Farrow"....."If you are right and he tries to involve me in anything, I will tell you, but I will not be used to spy against him," she replies.

Feodor does indeed seem to be the honest undeceptive gentleman she believes him to be. As their holiday in Barbados comes to a close, they agree to meet again - discreetly - in Paris. Here Feodor informs her that he told his superior General Golitsyn (Oskar Homolka) that he is building a relationship with her in the hopes of recruiting her as a KGB agent and that she must be frank and tell Loder of their meeting as well. "Let me teach you the first lesson about these little games," Feodor explains. "You must try to tell the truth as long as possible. That way, when times change and you have to lie, there is a great chance that you will be believed."

Judith has no taste for these Soviet cat-and-mouse games and yet she finds herself embroiled in them through her relationship with Feodor, a relationship she has no intention of pursuing since he is a married man and decidedly Marxist. "It is a good sign that we have many dialectic disagreements and yet get along so well together", Feodor exclaims. Perhaps so, but when Feodor's life becomes endangered, Judith must weigh her feelings for him against her loyalty to her own values.

The Tamarind Seed was released in theaters in the summer of 1974 and was received with critical acclaim. The film was chosen to be shown for a Royal Command Performance and returned over three times its $2.4 million budget at the box office.

Freddie Young's beautiful cinematography elevates the film beyond a standard espionage drama and makes you feel like you are watching an epic. Indeed, with location filming in London, Paris, Barbados, and Switzerland and John Barry's lush score (not to mention Wilma Reading's wonderful rendition of "Play it Again"), it could very well be classified as a dramatic spy epic.

Also in the cast are Sylvia Syms, Bryan Marshall, Kate O'Mara, and Celia Bannerman.

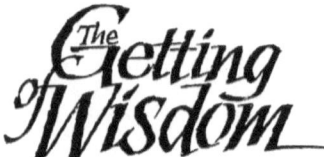

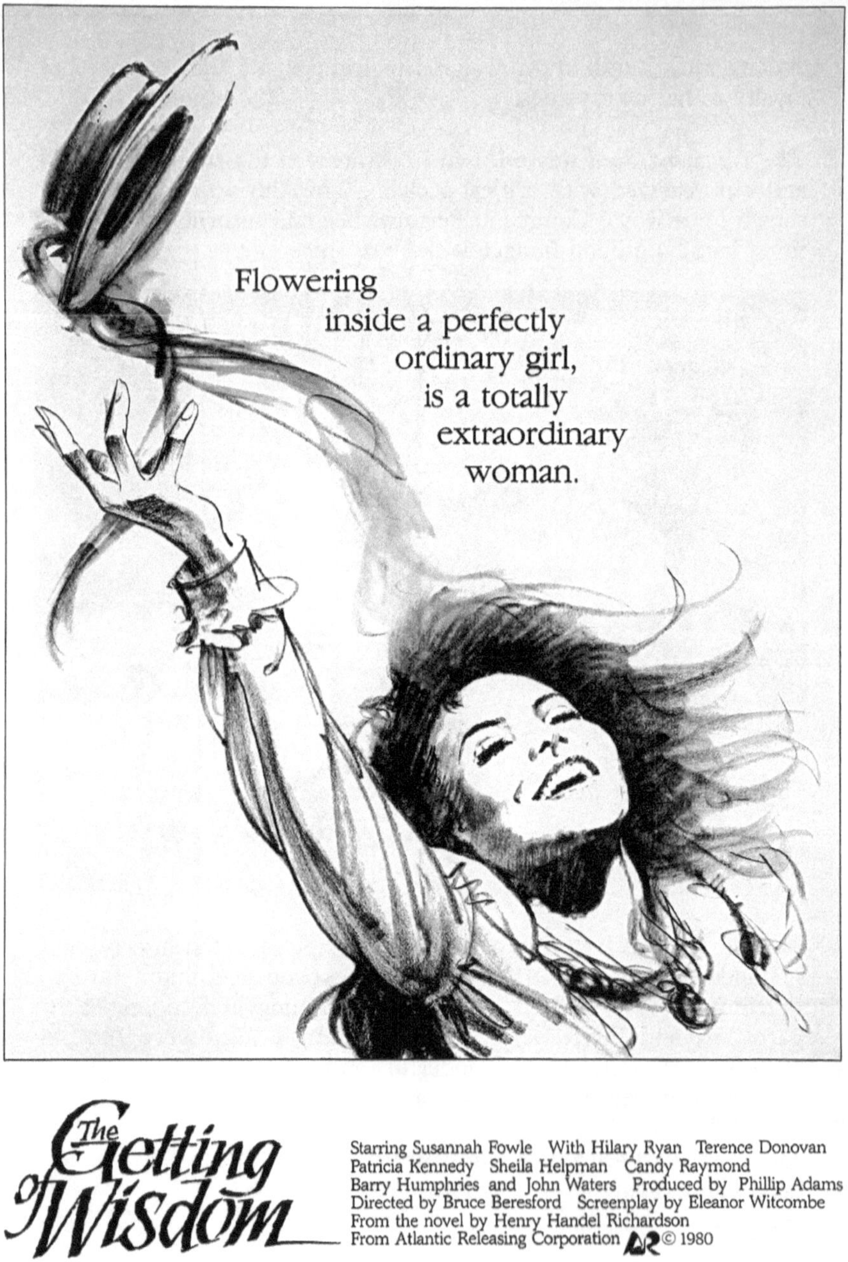
Flowering
inside a perfectly
ordinary girl,
is a totally
extraordinary
woman.
The Getting of Wisdom
Starring Susannah Fowle With Hilary Ryan Terence Donovan
Patricia Kennedy Sheila Helpman Candy Raymond
Barry Humphries and John Waters Produced by Phillip Adams
Directed by Bruce Beresford Screenplay by Eleanor Witcombe
From the novel by Henry Handel Richardson
From Atlantic Releasing Corporation © 1980

SOUTHERN CROSS FILMS (1977)

The Getting of Wisdom

"Wisdom is the principal thing; therefore get wisdom: and with all thy getting get understanding." - Proverbs 4:7

Laura Tweedle Rambotham, a delightfully awkward country girl, quickly discovers that at the exclusive Presbyterian Ladies' College in Melbourne, the getting of wisdom entails learning to conform to the behavior of your classmates, regardless of how stuffy and repressive their attitudes may be. It also means following the rules of socializing which she, unfortunately, has not fathomed. Nor will she by the conclusion of the film.

The Getting of Wisdom, a 1977 Australian production, follows the plight of the plain, unconventional Laura from her first day at school to her graduation from the college four years later. She arrives as a talented, imaginative, outspoken, and overly-confident thirteen-year-old and leaves as a pompous, irritable, and all the more insecure young woman.

One assumes that as the story unfolds the gradual transformation of an ugly duckling into a beautiful swan full of womanly graces will become apparent...but this does not happen. It is this aspect that made Henry Handel Richardson's classic 1910 novel "The Getting of Wisdom" so amusing. Director Bruce Beresford (*Driving Miss Daisy, Fried Green Tomatoes*), who had delighted in reading the novel as a teenager, wanted to keep this feature of the book when he adapted it to film.

So often our schoolgirl heroines are shy lovable lambs who are thrown amongst a pack of worldly-wise teenagers eager to toy with their innocence. But Laura is nothing of the kind. She is utterly assured of her own genius and anticipates settling into the school with relative ease. She hopes to impress her way to success both academically and socially but finds that no one appreciates a show-off. After her disappointing arrival - and her first cry - she begins to build an emotional armor constructed of suspicion, fear, and self-doubt.

As producer Philip Alford commented, "this ugly duckling never becomes a swan, not in the film, but she is taken under the wing of a swan". This swan, the elegant Evelyn Suitor, is one of the few people to have confidence in Laura and like her for who she is - a thoroughly selfish and crusty little girl. She gives Laura the opportunity to soften her heart and be more open and tender but Laura is blind to this. We can only hope that she loses her irritability and obstinacy later in life.

The Getting of Wisdom, a coming-of-age drama set in the early 1900s, touches on themes of romance, friendship, possessiveness, and acceptance. It was a film project very dear to Bruce Beresford's heart. He felt that there were many qualities in Laura's character that adolescents could relate to, which is quite true. The Ladies College, like most schools, is a microcosm of society where one can study and learn the rules of social intercourse. Unfortunately, the college's inmates are primarily shallow individuals.

"Everyone knows my mother is just a postmistress and does embroidery. I know what it is like not to have pocket money and beautiful clothes."

When Laura first arrives, she discovers that having a mother who works for a living is considered by her prestigious peers to be deeply shameful. Hence, she comes to downplay her homelife and searches instead for other means of gaining acceptance among her classmates. One method is through lies.

During her second year at the school, she concocts an illicit affair between herself and the handsome new minister Reverend Shepard (John Waters), a fantasy that she almost comes to believe herself. She basks in the fame this lie creates for her, but only for a short while. Once her deception is exposed, she is ostracized by all her classmates.... except Evelyn. This lovely senior takes a shine to the imaginative youngster. They share a common bond in Schubert and a skepticism towards authority figures, especially the kind that the

college is comprised of: uncompassionate self-righteous dictatorial teachers. These include the draconian headmistress Mrs. Gurley, the Reverend Strachey, and Miss Zielinski (Candy Raymond). Only Miss Chapman (Patricia Kennedy) shows an inkling of interest in the girls, but she does not garner their respect, hence they take no notice of her.

Like the book, *The Getting of Wisdom* is a mockery of class, a skillful study of human behavior brimming with shrewd humor, although this humor is much more subdued onscreen. The film is quite faithful to the novel except that Beresford chose to shift Laura's literary ambition to a musical one. Interestingly, he also added a strong sapphic undercurrent, making Laura not only emotionally but sexually attracted to Evelyn.

"What have those little monsters been telling you? Probably a pack of lies."

Evelyn represents the ideal that Laura is seeking (Beresford even hints that she represents Wisdom herself) and while there is satisfaction in being near to and loved by one so graceful it is not enough. Laura's worship of Evelyn and her infatuation with the exoticism that such a sophisticated older student would choose her as a companion eventually turns into obsession and possessiveness with Laura declaring, "I'll never share you with anybody!". In the novel, Evelyn takes this in her usual good humor and the two remain friends after their school years are over. However, in the film, Laura's jealousy turns to bitterness which is played out realistically in one of the many biting scenes in the picture.

16-year-old Susannah Fowle, a Melbourne schoolgirl, was selected from among 6,000 applicants to play the part of Laura. She had no prior acting experience and yet gives a passionate performance primarily through subtle gestures and facial expressions. Miss Fowle makes the character as dislikable as possible; in fact, much harsher than the book leads us to believe her to be. Only at times does Fowle permit us a glimpse at Laura's heart.

Hillary Ryan, who plays the part of Evelyn Suitor, was an American-born beauty whom Beresford had discovered in London. She should have gone on to have a long career in film but, instead, only made a handful of appearances in television.

John Waters is marvelous as the dashing but thoroughly boorish new minister and the rest of the cast is equally well-selected, particularly the schoolgirls. All of the teachers are merely caricatures overshadowed by the girls whom they teach. Barry Humphries aka Dame Edna, was an interesting if not daring choice for the role of the puritanical Reverand Strachey, and Sheila Helpmann (as fearsome looking as her brother Robert) is suitably impregnable as Mrs. Gurley.

The cinematography by Don McAlpine is beautiful and innovative. He featured an interesting selection of shots, mixing high and low angle compositions and wide-angles in place of close-ups.

The Getting of Wisdom is built up of short numerous episodic sequences. While the film unfolds slowly enough these individual scenes are played out too quickly. They are also filled with subtle touches which unfortunately are not emphasized enough to make the audience take notice of them. For example, in the finale, Laura's last-minute decision to play Schubert's Impromptu (a piece which she had played twice with Evelyn) at her piano recital instead of the announced Beethoven's Sonata No. 21 is a final touch of defiance to the school she is leaving and an acknowledgment that she is still besotted with Evelyn. The camera pans several teachers and students as Laura begins the piece, but it fails to show the reaction of Mrs. Hicks, the music teacher, whose expression would have clued the audience that Laura was not playing the intended composition. It takes repetitive viewings to fully appreciate scenes like this but if the audience is not hooked on the initial viewing then it is unlikely they will return to give the film a more thorough look.

Eleanor Whitcomb's screenplay fails to resolve Laura's character and this results in a loss of coherence of the entire film. At the conclusion of the picture we are left waiting for Laura to release the pent-up emotions of the past school year and toss her hat in the air as the poster suggests, but even this she does not do.

The sum of its parts simply does not equal a whole but overall, the pleasure derived from these individual scenes more than compensate for its inadequacies and *The Getting of Wisdom* is still worth a viewing.

Picture Credits

All images in this book are presented for editorial and educational purposes only. They include:

- **Scans of original movie posters and publicity photographs** issued by their respective production companies for promotional use. These materials are reproduced solely for commentary and review. The copyright for each image remains with its original rights holder. The name of the owning production company (e.g., Universal Pictures) is listed on the first page of each film review in the top left corner.
- **Screenshots taken from digital media** used to illustrate specific points within the film reviews. These screenshots are reproduced under the fair use doctrine of U.S. copyright law, for the purpose of criticism and commentary. All rights remain with the original copyright holders.

No commercial claim is made to the ownership of these images. Their inclusion is intended solely to support critical analysis and scholarly discussion.

Gainsborough Studios: 10; MGM/Amazon MGM Studios: 11-13, 24, 26-27, 41-42, 58-65, 92-95, 128-132, 141-145, 190-201; London Films: 17-19, 46-47; RKO/Concord Originals: 21-23, 156; Warner Brothers/Warner Bros. Discovery: 28-30, 32-39, 104, 106-107; Universal Pictures/Universal Studios: 48-57, 101-103, 133-134, 184-188, 215-219; Les Films Richebe: 66-70; Paramount Pictures/Paramount Global: 72-74, 114-116, 157-158, 161-163, 226-227; LenFilm Studios: 77-79; 20th Century Fox/The Walt Disney Company: 80-89, 119, 120, 122, 124, 136, 138-139, 220-224, 229-234; The Archers/Rank/StudioCanal: 96-99; Lux Film: 110,112-113; United Artists: 125-126; Columbia Pictures/Sony Pictures: 146, 148-153, 164-168, 175-176, 210-212, 214, 244-247; Walt Disney Pictures/The Walt Disney Company: 170-173, 179-180, 182-183, 204-208, 248-251; Les Films Du Carrosse: 235-237; EMI Films/StudioCanal: 242-243; Lorimar Films/Warner Brothers Discovery: 254-255; Southern Cross: 258-261. The following images were obtained from scans of movie magazines now in the public domain: 15,31,43,71,109,169, and 209.

Cover illustration: London Films. All rights reserved/Courtesy: The Silverbanks Pictures Archive; **Spine**: 20th Century Fox Film Corp/All Rights Reserved; **Back Cover**: 20th Century Fox Film Corp. All rights reserved/Courtesy: Everett Collection; MGM/Amazon MGM Studios. All rights reserved/Courtesy: Authors Collection.